THE HEART
OF THE QUR'AN

THE HEART
OF THE QUR'AN

AN INTRODUCTION TO ISLAMIC SPIRITUALITY

LEX HIXON

With a new foreword and commentary by
Neil Douglas-Klotz

Quest Books
Theosophical Publishing House

Wheaton, Illinois ♦ Chennai (Madras), India

The Theosophical Society acknowledges with gratitude the generous support of the Kern Foundation for the publication of this book.

The Theosophical Publishing House
P. O. Box 270
Wheaton, IL 60189-0270

Library of Congress Cataloging-in-Publication Data

Hixon, Lex.
The heart of the Qur'an: an introduction to Islamic spirituality / Lex Hixon; with a new foreword and commentary by Neil Douglas-Klotz.
    p.   cm.
Previously published as: Heart of the Koran.
ISBN 0-8356-0822-0
1. Sufism—Prayer books and devotions. 2. Koran—Meditations.
3. Koran—Appreciation. I. Douglas-Klotz, Neil. II. Hixon, Lex.
Heart of the Koran. III. Title.

BP189.62.H59 2003
297.1'226—dc21
                                                    2003047044

5   4   3   2   1   *   03   04   05   06   07   08

Printed in the United States of America

CONTENTS

FOREWORD

TO THE SECOND EDITION

This new edition of Lex Hixon's *Heart of the Koran* (now entitled *The Heart of the Qur'an*) comes at a very important time in the history of relations between Muslims and the rest of the world. Since the events of September 11, 2001, some media pundits and opinion makers in Western countries have demonized Islam as a religion of war and intolerance. In addition, an extremely small minority of Muslims have used the Qur'an to justify actions that go against both its spirit and letter. This is no more nor less than what has been done by fundamentalists in all of the major world religions. Such misinformation and fearmongering on both sides harm the overall cause of peace and understanding between members of what the Qur'an clearly calls one human family.

Likewise, on a personal level, we in the West have largely missed hearing the wisdom of the Qur'an, a wisdom that addresses contemporary, everyday life issues such as love, relationships, justice, work, and self-knowledge. We need this wisdom just as much as that of the Tao Te Ching, the Bhagavad Gita and the Dhammapada. That the latter are better known to Western readers than the Qur'an says more about the last hundred years of relations between the West and the Middle East than about the book's inherent value. As the reader will discover, the Qur'an has its own unique voice, one almost uniquely suited to the confusing swirl of information overload, materialism, and tangled relations between people that we all experience in the postmodern world.

Throughout his life, Lex Hixon explored the many ways in which the world's spiritual traditions are relevant to the modern condition. As a spiritual adventurer, he delved particularly deeply into Hinduism, Buddhism, and Islam and authored nine books. His first book, *Coming Home: The Experience of Enlightenment in the World's Traditions,* became a classic of comparative spirituality in 1978. His untimely passing in 1994 left a great gap in the ranks of those universal souls who have stood for love and compassion as the basis for life and religion. I had the pleasure of meeting Lex at a Sufi gathering not long before his passing and was impressed by both his heart and his humor.[1]

I have long recommended *Heart of the Koran* as the best introduction to the spirituality of the Qur'an and Islam. Almost uniquely, Hixon's versions regard the revelations of the Qur'an as actual spiritual experiences rather than mere words or ideas in which we are are asked to believe. There is every reason to believe that Muhammad and his early listeners understood the Qur'an in this way. Similarly, the mystics of Judaism and Christianity have maintained that we can best understand the Bible as the journey of a soul towards the divine—that is, as an account of living spiritual experiences, rather than as dogma or historical fact. Biblical translations that claim to be "literal" have largely obscured this aspect of revelation, while at the same time obscuring their own inherent bias. Unfortunately, translations of the Qur'an have suffered from the same tendency.

When *Heart of the Koran* was first released in 1988, some reviewers criticized Hixon's renditions as "not translation," or "a Sufi's view of the Qur'an." The first critique misunderstands entirely what translation, in the Qur'anic sense, actually is, and the second does not do justice to what Hixon accomplished. If we stay true to the literal meaning of the word *translation*—"to carry meaning across" the bridge of language—then Hixon's versions of Qur'anic passages recreate the "heard" and "felt" experience of Qur'an better than any other English translation.

Even though Lex Hixon worked from multiple previous English translations (rather than from the Arabic original), I find his expanded versions well within what the Arabic text allows. As we shall see, one can translate each Arabic word literally several different ways, according to the point of view and spiritual experience of the listener. Hixon's meditations follow in a long historical tradition of open translation and interpretation, based in the Arabic text's multileveled possibilties. A bit of background on this tradition will help readers understand how to best read and hear his meditations.

THE TRADITION OF INNER
TRANSLATION AND INTERPRETATION

Beginning in about the 8th century (C.E.), Ismaili and Sufi mystics developed an inner method of approaching the Qur'an called *ta'wil* (literally, "bringing back to the root"), which allowed for multileveled, experientially based interpretations of the Arabic text. They based their versions in the literal Arabic text; we could consider them "translation" in the current Western sense. In this way, each rendition could address the circumstances of particular Islamic communities as well as of particular mystics.

The Qur'an first mentions an "inner meaning" in Sura 18 (78, 82), in the story of the Prophet Musa (Moses) and Khidr.

In brief, Khidr, the mystical "green man" of the ancient Middle East, temporarily accepts Moses as his traveling companion and student, and then performs three strange acts. When Moses questions him about these, a behavior that Khidr had previously forbidden, Khidr gives him the *ta'wil,* or inner explanation of his actions.

As Qur'anic exegesis developed, scholars distinguished between *ta'wil* and *tafsir,* the "outer or more surface explanation of a passage." The great and recently departed Islamic scholar Annemarie Schimmel commented on the profundity of Qur'anic interpretation attempted by Islamic mystics and served by the Arabic language itself:

> [T]he mystics of Islam . . . knew that a deeper meaning lies behind the words of the text and that one has to penetrate to the true core. It may be an exaggeration that an early mystic supposedly knew 7,000 interpretations for each verse of the Qur'an, but the search for the never-ending meanings of the Qur'an has continued through the ages. The Arabic language has been very helpful in this respect with its almost infinite possibilities of developing the roots of words and forming cross-relations between expressions.[2]

While seven thousand different meanings may seem extreme to us today, we can look a bit closer at how this may have been possible. The basis for *ta'wil* lies in unique qualities of the Semitic languages that lead to ambiguity in the meaning of a particular text, much more so than with any Western language. The same passage not only can express different "times" in the Western sense (past, present, and future), but also different "spaces" (inner and outer). In addition, the ancient Semitic languages do not divide reality into the concepts westerners call *mind, body, psyche,* and *spirit.* Without going into detail, ancient Semitic languages construct reality in a very different way.

For these reasons, both Jewish and Islamic traditions of mystical interpretation point to the importance of individual letters and letter-combinations, each of which have their own meaning, feeling, energy, and direction. The Semitic languages depend upon a root-and-pattern system that allows one to translate a text literally in several different ways. In Islamic mysticism, this interpretive approach begins with a study of the letters of the alphabet themselves, which came to symbolize cosmic or universal patterns of energy.

For instance, the sixth Shia imam, Jafar-As-Sadiq (d. 765) writes in his Qur'anic commentary:

> In the first place, a thought surged in God, an intention, a will. The object of this thought, this intention, and this will were the letters from which God made the principal of all things, the indices of everything perceptible, the criteria of everything difficult. It is from these letters that everything is known.[3]

One principle of early Ismaili *ta'wil* was that the written Qur'an was but a reflection of the "Qur'an of Creation," which itself contained the source of all symbols of the sacred. The Qur'an itself supports this interpretation by mentioning the "Mother of the Book" (*ummil kitabi,* Sura 43:4) and the "Well-preserved Tablet" (*lauh mahfuz,* Sura 85:22), which remain with Allah in preexistence.

In relation to this interpretation, modern Islamic scholar Seyyed Hossain Nasr relates the practice of *ta'wil* to Islam's unified cosmology of humanity, nature, and the divine:

> In Islam the inseparable link between man [sic] and na-
> ture, and also between the sciences of nature and religion,
> is to be found in the Qur'an itself, the Divine Book which
> is the Logos or the Word of God . . . It is both the re-
> corded Qur'an (*al-Qur'an al-tadwini*) and the "Qur'an of
> Creation" (*al-Qur'an al-takwini*) which contains the "ideas"
> or archetypes of all things. That is why the term used to
> signify the verses of the Qur'an or *ayah* also means events
> occurring within the souls of men and phenomena in the
> world of nature.[4]

The same dense texture of sound and letter roots, branch-
ing into multiple layers of meaning, also helps to support the
notion of the inimitability of the Qur'an (its *ijaz*), which, according to Muslims, is proof of its divine character, as well as of
Muhammad's prophethood. On this basis, no one "literal" translation into any other language is actually possible. As Annemarie
Schimmel pointed out, this concept led to the problem of how
to transmit the contents of the Qur'an in lands where Arabic
was not the native language:

> It is the inadequacy of translations that has caused and
> still causes so many misunderstandings about the Qur'an
> and its message, especially when sentences are taken out
> of context and set absolute; for according to the Muslims'
> understanding, not only the words and *ayat* but also the
> entire fabric of the Qur'an, the interweaving of words,
> sound and meaning, are part and parcel of the Qur'an.[5]

Similarly, in prefacing his recent translations of the early
suras (or "chapters") of the Qur'an, Islamic scholar Michael Sells
points out that we need to consider the text in an oral, communal context in order to begin to understand it:

For Muslims, the Qur'an is first experienced in Arabic, even by those who are not native speakers of Arabic. In Qur'an schools, children memorize verses, then entire Suras. . . . As the students learn these Suras, they are not simply learning something by rote, but rather interiorizing the inner rhythms, sound patterns, and textual dynamics—taking it to heart in the deepest manner.

The Qur'anic experience is not the experience of reading a written text from beginning to end. Rather, the themes, stories, hymns and laws of the Qur'an are woven through the life of the individual, the key moments of the community, and the sensual world of the town and village.[6]

Hixon's renderings of important Qur'anic passages aim to communicate to readers some of the same experiential qualities that the text holds for practicing Muslims. As he says in the essay "Inside the Qur'an":

My attempt in these meditations is to dramatize what, from my own experience in the world of Islam, the sensitive Muslim person actually feels when reading the Holy Qur'an or listening raptly, sometimes without clear verbal comprehension, to the melodious chanting of the classical Arabic. (p. 28)

Like other Sufi mystics who practiced *ta'wil,* Hixon rejected the distinction of "literal" versus "figurative" meanings of the text. He considered such distinctions meaningless when we consider the ways in which Muslims actually experience the Qur'an. As he says in the same essay:

[M]y meditations stay very close to the basic level of meaning in the Holy Qur'an. For this fundamental stratum of significance I would not use the phrase "literal meaning," because this suggests some sort of *merely literal* meaning, which can be dismissed as relatively unimportant in relation to the high mystical quest. . . . What I would call the "basic meaning" of the verses is profoundly important. It forms the *basis* of Muslim practice and experiential belief, without which the various higher levels of mystical meaning would be nullified. (pp. 28–9)

Western readers may initially find the Qur'an's language both poetic and hard to grasp. Nowhere does the Qur'an present a straightforward, linear philosophy or simple account of events. It does not speak in short, pithy sayings or even isolate particular passages to particular ideas. Instead, it circles around themes and interweaves variations of them in a style more reminicent of music than prose. Both in Arabic as well as in Hixon's versions, what we hear is more like a multivoiced song or like jazz music. For this reason, I would recommend that readers at some point read aloud these versions in order to feel the flavor and sound of the text. This will bring one closer to the felt experience of the Qur'an in the original.

CHANGES IN THIS EDITION

At the publisher's request, I have reorganized the selections based on the major themes (and variations) that they express. As the reader will find, this is not a cut-and-dried affair, and many suras could easily be placed in several different themes. Wherever one approaches the Qur'an, one finds the same themes being repeated in slightly different ways, from different points of view, almost as though one were looking at a hologram. These themes are:

- the nature of divine Unity;

- the importance of just and ethical behavior;

- the experience of life as short and precious and that any day might be "judgment day";

- the view of nature and the whole continuing process of Creation as expressing the divine Unity;

- the essential harmony of all religious revelations; and

- guidance towards living a life of compassion and love.

Likewise, we can simultaneously see any particular passage as both prayer and meditation, as an affirmation of a way of life, and as a statement that attempts to express the ground of Being.

That westerners have usually not seen the Qur'an in this way in the past has much to do with past English translations, the earliest of which consciously attempted to make the Qur'an sound more "biblical" (that is, in the style of the King James English translation). Early English translators did some of this to win respect for the Qur'an in the West. Over the past century, both Christian and Jewish translators (like Martin Buber) have questioned whether the static quality of King James "biblical English" expresses anything of the immediacy of ancient Hebrew. This has led to newer, more Hebrew-like translations of the Torah (for instance, by Everett Fox and others).

Unfortunately, the revision of "Qur'anic English" did not generally keep pace with these developments. Like some previous biblical translations, Qur'anic versions have sometimes been hijacked by the more regressive elements of the tradition. For instance, we can find English translations that seem to consciously "translate out" the Qur'an's more universal aspects, perhaps to emphasize its uniqueness or its exclusivity.

As I mentioned earlier, because of the fluid nature of the Semitic languages with regard to basic Western concepts like time, space, and levels of reality, every translation of the Qur'an (or the Bible, for that matter) must choose its "viewpoint." Some, like Hixon's, reveal this viewpoint clearly. Others hide their agenda behind value-laden words like *literal, orthodox,* or *true* translation.

I have based my reorganization of Hixon's Qur'anic selections on thematic guides that he included in the first edition. A table of contents at the end of the book gives the titles and page numbers of the suras in their traditional order, and I would encourage the reader to experience the selections this way as well.

Although Hixon did not render all of the Qur'an, he did, true to his original intention and title, give us an approach to its heart. *Heart* means "living experiences," not sentimentality or emotionalism. While some recent translations of classical Sufi poets have made them into what I could call spiritual snack food, Hixon does not do this. I have not changed any of his language. Some readers may find the relentless reference to Allah as "He" objectionable, and in fact, there are ways of getting around the problem of gender-inclusive language in most suras. If Hixon were alive today, I would encourage him to review this area of his work. The Arabic of the Qur'an is already much more gender inclusive than any translation. For instance, even though the word *Allah* is grammatically male, the One's essence (*Dhat)* and attributes (*Sifat)* are both gendered female. Since English does not allow us to gender such ideas without personalizing them, it is difficult to convey this in any translation.

That Hixon was clear about the limitations of his translation is clear from the following statement he makes in his essay about the worldview of Islam:

> [W]hen we speak with humility and awe of Allah Most High, we are not referring to some deity, abiding in some heaven, circumscribed by some theology. We are invoking the only I Am, the only Consciousness, who composes whatever exists, and who is infinitely more comprehensive even than existence itself. We therefore cannot hold any theological or philosophical concepts about Allah, much less can we engage in any poetic descriptions of God or limit Him in any way, such as confining Him to one particular revelation.

In this regard, it is worth considering Hixon's view of himself as a Sufi or mystic. Most academic courses on religion (and most media accounts) consider Sufism as the "esoteric" or "mystical" side of Islam. Throughout his Qur'anic translations and accompanying essays, however, Hixon takes the view, shared by many Sufis, that a primary emphasis on love, justice, and the inner life, which has been labeled "Sufism" expresses, in fact, the original Islam. What came later, as a Persian Sufi teacher once told me, was "culture and politics."

> This mode of experiencing, or directly living, the Divine Love on earth is not primarily ethical or rational, but mystical. The life of constant, devoted service to fellow beings, which is the way of life revealed universally through all the prophets, is not a program of social action but a form of meditation on the Divine Love.

With regard to the remainder of the original edition, all of Hixon's companion essays have also been included here. His account of his own "spiritual adventures" vividly portrays the prerequisites necessary for any translator to approach the Qur'an—some experience of the states of awareness that the book relates. His essay on "Allah's Divine Song: Inside the Qur'an" goes into more detail about his approach to this project. I have moved his longest essay ("The Qur'anic Vision: Worldview of Islam") to an appendix, not because I judge it unimportant, but because I feel that, given the current arrangement, the reader can appreciate it better if it is read after delving into the Qur'anic selections themselves. In this essay, Hixon recaps some of the Qur'an's most important themes with examples from the text itself.

Finally, at the publisher's request, I have added some brief commentary before each major section, suggesting ways to hear Hixon's renditions with new ears. In general, I suggest that readers let go of habitual ways in which they may hear "spiritual" language and begin to come to grips with their own experiences of love, Creation, judgment, and justice, not in the past or future, but in the present moment. I certainly have had to do this repeatedly in approaching the Qur'an. It is only then that we begin to approach the immediacy of the Qur'anic revelation in its original Arabic, to which Hixon's wise and poetic renditions point us.

—DR. NEIL DOUGLAS-KLOTZ
(SAADI SHAKUR CHISHTI)
Edinburgh Institute for Advanced Learning
Edinburgh, Scotland
February 2003

PART ONE
Islam and Its Spirituality

Chapter One

UNDERSTANDING ISLAM

(PREFACE TO THE ORIGINAL EDITION)

Neither as Christians or Jews, nor simply as intellectually responsible individuals, have members of Western civilization been sensitively educated or even accurately informed about Islam. For more than a thousand years, obvious and subtle prejudices against the way of love and wisdom called *Islam* have been instilled into European cultures. Even some persons of goodwill who have gained acquaintance with Islam continue to interpret the reverence for the Prophet Muhammad and the global acceptance of his message as the inexplicable survival of the zeal of an ancient desert tribe. This view ignores fourteen centuries of Islamic civilization, burgeoning with artists, scholars, statesmen, philanthropists, scientists, chivalrous warriors, philosophers, saints, and mystics, as well as countless common men and women of devotion and wisdom from almost every nation on the planet.

The coherent world civilization called Islam, founded in the vision of the Qur'an, cannot be regarded simply as the product of individual and national ambition, supported by historical accident. This vast spiritual community, consisting today of more than one billion persons, can only be understood as the result of the holy life of Muhammad. Islam will continue to blossom throughout the future of the planet, awakening human beings to the true nobility of the soul and to the sublimity of its Source, providing a disciplined and harmonious way of life for a large segment of humanity.

The history of Islam is not free from intolerance, injustice, and other chronic distortions of the human spirit. Neither is Christian history free from such distortions. But these sobering facts cannot dim the wonder of twenty centuries of commitment flowing from the inspired life of Jesus, and fourteen centuries of commitment flowing from the inspired life of Muhammad. The power of authentic revelation cannot be understood simply in terms of political and cultural history. There exists one ultimate Source from which the entire universe is harmoniously flowing. This sublime and healing knowledge dawns within the human heart and mind, individually and collectively, through contact with clear channels of truth and love, such as Moses, Jesus, and Muhammad.

There is no way that I can dispel every false or incomplete impression about Islamic spirituality, which the prospective readers of this book may hold. Instead, I ask you to experiment by temporarily suspending any negative judgments. Simply assume Islam to be among the great wisdom traditions of humanity, all of which are worthy of fundamental respect. This will create an attitude of openness in which the reader can drink from the illuminating fountain of the Holy Qur'an.

All Muslims place the Qur'an at the center of their life, faith, and practice, for every word of this scripture was received by the Prophet Muhammad during the exalted state of consciousness through which the Source of the universe speaks directly to humanity. The revealed words of this Qur'an, when experienced reverently and profoundly, are not relics from the past but exist in a timeless present, communicating as vividly as when they were first uttered. If we are patient and concentrate, we will discover that these words of Allah often refer with mysterious precision to whatever historical or personal situation presents itself to us.

The encounter with the Qur'an as living revelation is the single thread from which all the dimensions of Muslim spiritual life and civilization are woven. After sharing this precious encounter for even a few moments—an experience that the present book attempts to make possible for the general reader of English—we can never again be satisfied with a superficial understanding of the Prophet Muhammad and the rich heritage of Islam. We now feel kinship with the vast spiritual family of devout Muslim men and women that extends throughout the world.

It is my hope that readers of this book will be stimulated to turn or return to various scholarly translations of the Holy Qur'an, and even to the Arabic original, with openness and new inspiration. This is not a treatise *about* Islam, written from the perspective of another religious tradition or from a supposedly neutral academic standpoint. This is a meditation on the Holy Qur'an that has been generated from within the mystical embrace of Islam. Therefore, *Heart of the Koran* is an offering to the Muslim world as well as to members of other cultures and traditions who have an intellectual curiosity or a spiritual desire to learn about Islam from within.

The Arabic word *Islam* simply means "surrender"; Muslims are those who consciously and constantly surrender their lives to the single Source of the universe. This is the practice of living prayer that enables humanity to realize balance, responsibility, freedom, ecstasy, and peace. May we all experience such surrender.

Chapter Two

SPIRITUAL ADVENTURES:
DREAM AND PILGRIMAGE

*H*eart of the Koran presents meditations on 991 verses of the Holy Qur'an, the Arabic Book of Books, which records in 6,666 verses the Divine Words spoken by God directly through His beloved servant, Muhammad. I have composed these interpretations of 148 Qur'anic passages to encourage practitioners of other sacred traditions, as well as independent students of culture, to encounter the rich meaning and uplifting beauty that Muslims on all levels of spiritual maturity experience daily as they read, chant, and pray from the Holy Scripture of Islam. A word-for-word translation of the Qur'an in any language cannot begin to suggest the beauty and magnitude of meaning found in the Arabic original by the devout believers, the profound scholars, and the marvelous mystics who have flowered so abundantly throughout the fourteen centuries of Islamic tradition. I have attempted in *Heart of the Koran* to depart from literal, scholarly English translations and to explore in mystical and poetic language Qur'anic passages that clearly present the central teachings of Islam.

Sheikh Muzaffer, renowned leader of the Halveti-Jerrahi

Dervish Order in Istanbul, once remarked to me that there are as many levels of meaning to the Qur'an as there are words, even as there are letters, in the Holy Book. This statement served as a powerful initiation into the mystery of the Qur'an, for from that moment my attitude toward this monumental world scripture began to be transformed. I no longer experienced the text of the Qur'an as a flat, two-dimensional surface, the way I had during graduate study in world religions, but as a multidimensional tapestry of mystical teaching.

The transition from the academic study of religion to the inward experience, or practice, of its living tradition is unique in every individual case. My own journey was not solitary but carefully guided by two powerful Islamic figures, Bawa Muhaiyaddeen from Sri Lanka and Sheikh Muzaffer Ozak from Istanbul. I assimilated subtle truths about Islam not only from these two perfected human beings but also from their Eastern and Western disciples, who form spiritual communities of great purity and intensity that demonstrate esoteric understanding in daily life. Both these Sufi Masters made comments about the manuscript of *Heart of the Koran*, not primarily through words but through the mysterious gestures common among mystics. Bawa Muhaiyaddeen put the first typescript in his bed, eight years ago, as if to keep it concealed until the right time. Sheikh Muzaffer placed a later version of the manuscript on his head after my meditation on Sura 103 was translated for him, and exclaimed in Turkish, "This is the Holy Qur'an."

THE PRACTICE OF ISLAM

To be Muslim in the universal sense is to be one who longs to turn completely toward the ultimate Source, in Arabic called

Allah. Who is and who is not truly Muslim is a secret known only to Allah Most High. No human being can judge another concerning this most intimate experience of affirming and returning to the One Reality. The question of where a person stands along the exalted way of Islam, of whether one practices the five times daily prayer, or even which prophet one follows among the many sent by Allah, can only be a subject for dialogue between the soul and its All-Merciful Lord. There can be no compulsion or persecution in authentic Islam. Whoever affirms and longs to return to the ultimate Source of the universe is the beloved spiritual sister or brother of the true Muslim. Since every soul is a ray from the Divine Light, this longing to turn and to return is the secret essence of each person. Thus all humanity, even all Creation, is Muslim.

Once the universal nature of Islam is understood as the religion natural to the human soul taught by God through prophets sent to every nation in history, we can better appreciate the beauty of the *Shariah*, the particular holy way of life demonstrated by the Prophet Muhammad.

The *Shariah* is the sharply focused dimension of Islam, where every aspect of spiritual practice and daily life is gracefully choreographed. Every movement of ablution and prayer, performing the pilgrimage, fasting, and giving alms is rich with meaning and power, for it was first made by the Prophet of Allah. Through my close friendship with Sheikh Muzaffer, I have been able to glimpse the union of the two dimensions of Islam—universal, all-embracing, ecstatic love, and the careful precision of a deeply sanctified and morally committed daily life. Sheikh Muzaffer demonstrated the unity of these two modes: the *Haqiqah*, or way of ultimate truth, and the *Shariah*, or path of religious discipline.

The most exalted mystical love and knowledge, which

perceive the whole universe constantly returning into the Source, and even entirely merged in the Source, can be profoundly expressed through the faithfulness and precision of daily religious disciplines. In the case of historical Islam, this means to live life in detail as the beloved Prophet lived it, as documented by the Holy Qur'an and by the Prophet's own oral tradition. Such harmony between the vision of the all-transcending truth and the humane activity of a dedicated life in society is the richest possible experience. This experience is, in fact, the fullness of being human. Personal and cultural being, the being of the universe, and the Source of Being are thus mysteriously integrated.

Sheikh Muzaffer was known for the radiance of spirit with which he performed the daily prayers of Islam. In the simple, powerful movements of his prostrations, which are the same movements practiced by all Muslims, there shone forth the marvelous correspondence between the open expanse of Divine Light and the responsible earthly life of humanity. One could be awakened to a more profound understanding of Islam simply by seeing Sheikh Muzaffer at prayer in his small shop beneath the grapevines in the booksellers' section of the Istanbul bazaar. In 1985, this Grand Sheikh breathed his last breath, forehead on his prayer carpet in prostration, while making midnight prayers in his home beside the Sea of Marmara.

The practice of the *Shariah*, or the path of religious discipline, links together the highest saints and the simplest believers from every Islamic culture in the world into a single family. No one can experience the refreshing ablutions and peaceful prayers of Islam without sensing the quiet elation and deep unity shared by this vast spiritual family, far below the surface of cultural tensions. Repeating the Holy Name of Allah as one rinses the hands, mouth, nostrils, face, forearms, and feet three times with cool water in the traditional ablutions before prayer, one feels not

only surprising physical refreshment, but also far-reaching purification of thought and emotion.

To face in the direction of the holy city of Mecca, allowing
the entire body and mind to flow into the prostrations of Muslim prayer, awakens the sense of plunging directly into the Divine
Presence. The physical space before one disappears, and the rich
blackness of the Ka'bah, the sacred shrine in Mecca, appears mysteriously to the spiritual sensibility. One is then drawn closer
and closer to this imageless and radiant blackness until all forms—
one's own body as well as the universe itself—merge into the
unfathomable Divine Mystery. This holy mystery is then recognized as the one Power performing the prayers and receiving the
prayers, as both the act of praise and that which is being praised.
Although not always experienced by the surface mind, this mystic unity is the essence of the Islamic prayers into which the
whole being of the Muslim plunges five times every day, not
merely to fulfill a ritual requirement but to swim joyfully and
peacefully in the ocean of Divine Love. The prayers are the union
of *Shariah* and *Haqiqah*, the merging of formal religious practice with the mysterious truth of unity that transcends all forms
and all traditions. During the course of the five prayer periods
every day, each of which is brief but whose cumulative effect
pervades life completely, the opening chapter of the Holy Qur'an,
the Sura *Fatihah*, is repeated some forty times. In addition to
these daily repetitions, this sura is repeated whenever one passes
the tomb of a saint, when giving thanks after a meal, or when
seeking the protection of God from various physical or spiritual
dangers. Over a thousand times every month, the illuminating
energy of this fundamental prayer from the Holy Qur'an is inwardly invoked by the Muslim, until it becomes a constant
ringing presence in the deeper regions of awareness.

According to the oral tradition of the Prophet, the entire

power of the Qur'an is contained in this brief sura, the chanting of which allows one to participate in the mysterious descent of the Holy Qur'an to earth, the process by which the ultimate Source transmitted Divine Words to humanity through the perfectly human body and mind of the Prophet of Allah. This mystical participation of our entire being in the descent of the Divine Words is what *Heart of the Koran* attempts to illuminate for English readers in every culture of the modern world.

Early in our friendship, I was sitting with Sheikh Muzaffer one late afternoon in the ancient Bayazit Mosque of Istanbul. It was during Ramadan, the Islamic month of fasting that commemorates the Prophet's own retreat to the mountain cave where he first experienced the descent of the Qur'an. We were enjoying together the poignant beauty of a *hafiz*, an Islamic cantor, singing the Holy Qur'an from memory, verses which he had repeated since childhood and which had become as natural to him as his own breathing. Gazing into the great domed space, radiant and peaceful, surrounded by this living revelation in pure sound, I was granted the vision of a translucent emerald mosque, above even the highest heaven. There were no human figures visible, only a vast Qur'an whose letters radiated light and whose pages turned gracefully as it spontaneously chanted itself. Later, the Sheikh confirmed to me that this had been an authentic mystical experience, not simply the product of creative imagination.

The penetration of my awareness into the deeper levels of meaning of the Holy Qur'an—teachings that are confirmed and safeguarded by the initiatory lineages, the mystical Orders of Islam—came initially through an exhilarating but completely natural experience that unfolded one spring morning in a peaceful house near New York City, where a large window overlooks a garden and a river.

This experience occurred one month after I had become the intimate friend of Sheikh Muzaffer. Our first encounter had been extremely powerful—a meeting of mind and heart that lasted for six days and nights. When the Grand Sheikh of the Halveti-Jerrahi Order returned to Istanbul from New York, I began to read the interpretation of the Qur'an by Professor A. J. Arberry and, following the instructions of my Sheikh, to repeat seven hundred times every day the central Islamic affirmation *la ilaha illa'llah,* signifying: "There is nothing worthy of worship other than the ultimate Source of the universe, whose most holy Arabic name is *Allah.*" According to the mystical tradition of Islam, this affirmation implies that nothing exists apart from Allah, the Most High, and that every being is a ray of light and power from the ever-present Source.

During this period of spiritual preparation, I spent one evening a week with Sheikh Muzaffer's American dervish community, drinking black tea and intensely chanting the Divine Names until dawn. I had been informed that the higher teachings in the contemplative Orders of Islam were expected to come directly through dreams. Looking back at the process, I find the only surprise was that I happened to be awake when the transcendent dream occurred.

WITH THE PROPHET MUHAMMAD IN PARADISE

My soul departs its earthly body and is taken in a waking dream to Paradise. Led by a loving guide, it discovers vast, radiant gardens filled with joyous beings of light, who are engaged in countless forms of whirling, chanting, and silent contemplation.

Though overwhelmed with the beauty of Paradise, my soul wishes to understand the whole picture, and therefore asks its

guide where the fires of Hell are to be found. Smiling, the guide
replies: "Dear friend, there is no separate realm that you call Hell."

My soul, steeped in the revelation of Islam, responds immediately: "But we read in the Holy Qur'an that those who deny
Allah will suffer in Hell eternally." The beloved guide replies
firmly: "But you read again and again in the Holy Qur'an that
Allah is all-compassionate and all-merciful. How could an all-
compassionate Power create a realm expressly designed for beings
to suffer even for an instant, much less for eternity?"

This response startles and intrigues my soul, but it remains
unconvinced. Perceiving this, the guide continues: "What is
taught in the mystic tradition about the person who, even once,
repeats with utmost sincerity *la ilaha illa'llah*—the ultimate
Source alone is worthy of worship?" Joyously my soul replies:
"Such a one is counted among the blessed and after death awakens immediately into Paradise."

"Good!" exclaims the guide, "and since all souls are rays
from the Divine Light, the essence of every being is this affirmation that Allah alone is worthy of worship, and all beings awaken,
after the sleep of death, directly into Paradise."

My soul is exhilarated by this profound explanation, but
because of its deep commitment to the words of the Qur'an, it
still hesitates to accept the truth that there is no separate realm
called Hell. The beloved guide sees this hesitation and offers my
soul the final solution to its doubts: "My dear friend, it is true
that when a soul who has not practiced the life of loving submission to Allah reaches Paradise, it cannot bear the intense radiance
here, so falls asleep again and dreams of Hell. Hellfire is simply
the purifying radiance of Paradise. And all dreams, even dreams
of eternal damnation, are but momentary. These dreaming souls
soon awaken into Paradise, fully purified and joyously praising
the All-Merciful One." The explanation now complete, my soul

feels the full coherence and power of this marvelous truth, the all-merciful nature of Allah.

However, this mystical teaching deepens the soul's longing to understand completely, so almost at once a profound question arises: "Revered guide, if the experience of Hell is but a dream, may not the experience of Paradise—its dancing maidens, its flowing streams, its radiant dervishes—may not all this be a dream as well?" The guide responds with delight: "Ah, my dear, dear friend, you have guessed the secret. Paradise, too, is a dream. But it is Allah's perfect dream, totally unlike the fragmentary and confused dreams experienced by earthly beings."

These words kindle the ecstasy of mystical knowledge in my soul, and it realizes that this unsurpassable guide is none other than the Prophet Muhammad, may the peace and blessing of Allah always be upon him. And in this state of holy exultation the soul becomes bold enough to question the Prophet of Allah: "Beloved guide, are you, too, a dream, telling me that Hell and Paradise are dreams?" The most excellent of guides responds instantly and with great power: "I am the dream key to the dream lock of the dream door that opens into the treasure of Divine Love, which alone is not a dream."

A mystical door opens through the spiritual potency of these words. My soul enters and is lost in the treasure of love. The dream of Paradise disappears. All that remains is the profound sense of Allah's own resonance, the silent thunder of *Allah, Allah, Allah.* From this primordial holy sound all the universes are being born, and into it they are disappearing again.

Suddenly, my soul finds itself once more in the radiant divine dream called Paradise. The beloved guide takes my soul in his arms and holds it in a tender embrace, saying: "Now you know that we are inseparable." My soul looks down and sees its own form no longer as a body of light, but as a body fully composed of Divine Love. And then, hand in hand, the two who are one stroll through the radiance of Paradise, joyously praising the All-Merciful One.

The guide now leads my soul to a vast window at the border of Paradise. From here the soul can look out upon Allah's Creation, both in its cosmic sweep and in its intimate detail. Gazing at this awesome display, my soul suddenly feels intense nostalgia: "Beloved guide, can one ever return to the created universe from Paradise?"

Smiling once more, the guide replies: "There is no separate realm, which you call Creation." Through the spiritual potency of these words, my soul perceives immediately that this is not a window but a huge spherical mirror that surrounds Paradise on all sides. When the elements of Paradise are reflected in the immense curvature of this mirror, they appear as the elements of Creation. The flowing streams of Paradise, when reflected, appear as the streams of all sentient life. When the dancing maidens of Paradise are reflected, they appear as the life-bearing planets. When the dervishes of Paradise are reflected, they appear as precious human souls. The entire universe is simply the reflection of a divine dream.

While contemplating this marvelous correspondence between Creation and Paradise, my soul catches sight of its own earthly form, standing in a house on a spring morning, gazing across a river. "Beloved guide, I have the vivid sensation of being in two places at once." Again smiling, the guide replies: "My dear friend, when you look at your face in a mirror, do you really imagine that you are in two places at once? Are you not always where your original form is?"

Once again the words of the guide carry initiatory power, and my soul, when it looks back to catch another glimpse of its earthly form, perceives all Creation as a reflection of its own face. Overwhelmed by this realization, my soul turns to its guide only to see Paradise, and even the beloved guide himself, as a reflection of its own face. Nothing disappears. All Being, in brilliant detail, is simply perceived as one face.

Then a voice is heard emanating from rivers, gardens, and dervishes of Paradise, as well as from all the crystal-clear facets of Creation: "Do you accept this pure love in all its forms as Allah's embrace?" And not simply my soul but all souls answer simultaneously, "Yes, forever!"

The Jerrahi dervish who translated my account of this experience from English to Turkish for Sheikh Muzaffer told me that certain secret oral teachings of his Order were clearly alluded to in the dream, confirming my own conviction that this waking dream was a mystical transmission of the way of Pir Nureddin Jerrahi, the consummate saint of love from Istanbul. Sultan Muhammad Nureddin Jerrahi disappeared from physical eyes in 1721, yet he continues to radiate as a powerful ray of light from the ever-present Source. I once asked Sheikh Muzaffer, who was the nineteenth leader of the Jerrahi Order in direct succession from its august founder, what special divine gift this saint had brought to humanity. Why had he been born? Muzaffer Efendi replied: "For love, for love, for love." He then explained that Pir Nureddin had demonstrated the mystic way of melting, evaporating, and disappearing into Allah, only to reappear again as Divine Love itself.

Based on the guiding power and inner permission granted by this dream, I have meditated on the Holy Qur'an both as a teaching and as a direct expression of mystic love. Allah Most High is the Source of Love. Souls are the lovers of love. Creation, which is the reflection of the divine dream called Paradise, is Allah's embrace. Hellfire is the mercifully purifying radiance of Allah. The Divine Revelation shining the prophets is the path of love. The Prophet Muhammad is the dream key, abiding in the secret heart of all humanity, which is the dream lock. The Holy Qur'an, in all its mysterious facets, is the dream door that opens to the treasure of Divine Love that alone is not a dream. Upon truly hearing the Divine Words of the Holy Qur'an, that ultimate door opens.

One cannot present the Qur'an in this fashion solely through efforts of scholarship or accomplishments of poetic art, but only through the love of Allah. Divine Love and Divine Knowledge are focused through the inner guidance of the Nur Muhammad, the Muhammad of Light, the preexistent *Logos* as understood by Islam. This light shines before all worlds and is manifested through the beloved Muhammad of Arabia, as through all 124,000 prophets that the Islamic tradition teaches were sent by Allah Most High, beginning with Adam and extending with perfect continuity through Abraham, Moses, and Jesus.

PILGRIMAGE TO MECCA AND MEDINA

In keeping with the mysterious way that spiritual experience progresses, soon after I had completed the first draft of this book, I was blessed to make the traditional *hajj* of Islam—the pilgrimage to Mecca to circumambulate the Holy Ka'bah, the symbolic earthly focus of the Divine Presence and the center of spiritual power and inspiration for the Islamic world. Sheikh Muzaffer's party of Turkish and American dervishes traveled from New York City to Saudi Arabia, where some three million Muslim pilgrims from almost every nation on the planet gather during a single week. By the Will of Allah, this potent sacrament of pilgrimage into the desert of mystery and power was made easy for us, compared with the terrible hardship and danger faced by pilgrims even as recently as forty years ago.

All Muslims intend to make the pilgrimage to two holy cities in Arabia, Mecca and Medina, at least once in their lifetimes. It was while residing in his native city of Mecca that the Prophet Muhammad, at the age of forty, began to receive the revelation of the Holy Qur'an. The Prophet remained in Mecca for the next thirteen years, courageously transmitting the Divine Words and meeting with nonviolence the most violent and bitter persecution from the leaders of the city. After his small group of followers had undergone much suffering, Muhammad finally received permission from Allah to retire to Medina, several hundred miles distant. He lived on earth only ten more years, during which time he received permission from Allah to engage in nineteen battles to defend the freedom of the newly revealed religion. During this exalted period of his residence at Medina, Arabia embraced Islam. Medina is thus a center of intense spiritual fruitfulness. The noble Muhammad informed his companions that, as the ancient Prophet Abraham had sanctified Mecca by constructing the original Ka'bah, or House of Allah, there, just so had he, the contemporary prophet in the lineage of Abraham, specially sanctified Medina with the full revelation of Divine Love.

We arrived in Medina by jet in the Muslim year 1400, exactly fourteen centuries after the Holy Prophet had arrived there by camel caravan. The next morning we were to make our dawn prayers in the vast mosque that surrounds the Tomb of the Prophet, located at the humble desert dwelling where the Messenger of God lived his final years of spiritual exultation. I fell asleep at two in the morning, and dreamed that I was permitted to ask the Prophet Muhammad one question about the highest teaching of Islam.

While dreaming, I formulated the question: "What is meant by the passages in the Holy Qur'an that reveal that through every thought and action, each being in the universe is spontaneously praising Allah?" I was not able to see the Holy Prophet in my dream, but felt completely confident that my question was being conveyed to him. Only later did I discover that Sheikh Muzaffer had been keeping a nightlong vigil before the Holy Tomb.

Suddenly I awoke. I had been asleep only an hour, but was in such an intense state of wakefulness that I could not even lie down again. The answer to my dream question came to me at this moment of clarity and perfect silence in the desert oasis of Medina, through the Arabic words of a short chapter from the Holy Qur'an, Sura 112, which reveals the all-embracing oneness and inconceivable completeness of Allah the Most High. This sura teaches that the ultimate Source is not brought into being by any other power, nor does any being come into being separate from the all-embracing One. The entire universe is composed of the attributes of Allah praising the essence of Allah.

These highly compressed Arabic verses did not just flash through my mind, but entered my whole being with tremendous impact. As I took ablutions before offering formal prayer, tears of gratitude flooded my eyes. The question had been asked from the Holy Qur'an and the answer had flowed through the potent Arabic words of the Qur'an. When I presented my dream to Sheikh Muzaffer for interpretation, as is the practice in the Jerrahi Order of Dervishes, he immediately replied: "You are fortunate indeed. This is a very good dream. It means that your pilgrimage has been accepted." Everyone present felt the transcendent power of these words spoken through the Sheikh.

The spiritual atmosphere of Medina is pure sweetness. Tears of love flow easily at the Tomb of the Prophet and at the tomb of his beloved daughter, Fatima, the holy mother of the faithful.

One American dervish inhaled waves of rose fragrance, tradi-
tionally in Islam the scent of spiritual perfection, while praying
where the Prophet of Allah used to offer his prayers. But traveling to the holy city of Mecca is to enter an entirely different
sacred atmosphere. The delicate and intimate mystery of Medina
is replaced by an almost terrifying sense of vastness and power.
Medina is the transport of love, while Mecca is the all-consum-
ing fire of knowledge.

The overwhelming presence in Mecca of some three million pilgrims, dressed in white shrouds, dead to the world and
facing Allah alone, dramatizes the mystical function of the pilgrimage, which allows us, while we are still on earth, to experience
death and the Day of Resurrection. During this process, the pilgrims are stripped naked on every level of their being by the
awesome Lord of Power. Millions of us camped in tents together
in the valley of Mina, where, in ancient times, the Prophet
Abraham faced the supreme test from Allah: the Divine Command to sacrifice his own beloved son. Gazing from rocky and
barren hillsides, we could see white tents stretching for many
miles. The spiritual mood was intense, as each pilgrim inwardly
contemplated Abraham's willingness to offer to God what was
most precious to his own heart.

We spent the traditional sunrise to sunset on the barren
rock of Mount Arafat, where the Prophet received the final revelation of the Holy Qur'an shortly before his physical death.
Under a few feet of shade on the dusty roadside in 115-degree
heat, I clung desperately to my prayer beads, repeating again
and again the Arabic words indicating that Allah is the single
Source of all Being and Muhammad is His Messenger. I felt that
my body and mind had been consumed by the overwhelming
brightness of Arafat. The spiritual affirmation, *la ilaha ill'allah
Muhammad rasul Allah,* was all that I had left.

Near the potent hour of sunset, Sheikh Muzaffer began to chant the prayer that invokes one thousand and one Divine Names, including the more commonly known ninety-nine names of Allah. This text was the message, revealed by the Archangel Gabriel to the Prophet of Allah, that he no longer needed to wear armor into battle. The Sheikh remarked, "Hearing this, you will never need armor again. There will come a time when you will need nothing at all."

Countless vehicles and pilgrims on foot streamed by us as we sat on thin grass mats in the late afternoon sunlight, its harshness softened into golden radiance through the desert dust raised by this nomadic family of three million. Riding home at night on top of our bus, I observed the most impossible tangle of traffic. People left their vehicles, went shopping, prepared and enjoyed their dinners without the slightest forward progress. Yet all were profoundly content. Their pilgrimage was now almost complete.

The next night we made our third and farewell *Tawaf*, consisting of seven circumambulations of the Holy Ka'bah. In the center of the huge white marble courtyard within the grand mosque in Mecca stands the cubic structure, covered with rich black cloth, that represents the axis of the world. Islamic tradition tells us that this sacred cube was first built by the Prophet Adam, was constructed again after millennia by the Prophet Abraham, and was then renewed and rededicated to the One God by the Prophet Muhammad. The inspiration of this vast and powerful prophetic lineage tangibly irradiates the atmosphere.

Since the ever-present Source is formless, there are no images within or around this shrine. Its radiant blackness symbolizes the unimaginable holy mystery. The Divine Radiance here is too intense to experience as light. The mystic blackness is more luminous than that which exists beneath the surface of the sun.

Lost in an ecstatic whirlpool of several hundred thousand human forms, we are drawn closer and closer toward the axis of Being where the Divine Transcendence fully intersects with our planetary dimension of existence. Muslims from cultures throughout the earth are facing toward this center of the world, the Holy Ka'bah, as they perform their daily prayers, thereby transforming the entire planet into a sacred mosque.

Barefoot on cool marble, in the hours after midnight, we are swept round and round this central pole of manifestation. There are no tears, no insights, no visions. The essence of reality revealed here is too transcendent to be rendered into the language of the senses, mind, or heart. Only the secret soul knows what is here, that reality that neither words nor even experience can express. The true Ka'bah is none other than the diamond essence of the soul, the Muhammad of Light, the Logos who is simply Allah knowing Allah.

Following this final *Tawaf,* we returned as pure as newborn infants to the school outside Mecca where we were staying. We drank tea, performed the dawn prayers, and plunged into sleep. I dreamed for hours that I was repeating *"Ya Salaam, Ya Salaam, Ya Salaam"*—one of the ninety-nine Qur'anic Names of Allah meaning, *Thou All-Peaceful One.* Drifting into the waking world, I could see my pilgrim brothers asleep on their mats around me and could clearly perceive that Divine Peace was descending not just upon me, but upon them and the whole world. Entering into dream again, I would continue to intone with my whole being, *Ya Salaam.*

I awoke profoundly refreshed. My companions told me that I looked different. When I presented my dream to Sheikh Muzaffer, his comment was, "This confirms that your pilgrimage has been accepted, and Allah is sending you His Salaams."

Chapter Three

ALLAH'S DIVINE SONG:
INSIDE THE QUR'AN

The Holy Qur'an, we must always remember, does not contain the human speech and thought of the Prophet Muhammad, but is the Divine Song of power and love sung directly by Allah, the ultimate Source of the universe, through the personal, cultural, and spiritual being of His Prophet. The Holy Qur'an, in its depth, is direct revelation, regardless of whatever historical studies are made of its surface. No meditation upon the Qur'an, no matter how strong the inspiration or how broad the scholarship, could begin to equal the Arabic original, simply because the Arabic Qur'an remains in the realm of revelation. This is a living revelation, occurring afresh each time the Holy Qur'an is sung or chanted, for these Arabic words are the actual resonance of Allah Most High, and thus they transmit healing, protecting, transforming, and illuminating power directly from the Source.

Heart of the Koran attempts to suggest the spiritual richness of the original text in a dignified contemporary English. The title *Inspirations from the Holy Qur'an* was suggested by Sheikh Muzaffer, who reviewed and approved the manuscript, to make clear to the reader that this is a book of personal inspiration that lays no claim to scholarly or religious authoritativeness.

This project began unexpectedly as I was preparing a radio documentary on Islam. I experimented with my own free rendering of the opening chapter of the Qur'an, working from a literal English translation. An Arabic scholar heard my reading over the radio and inquired after its origin, explaining that he considered it the most evocative English version of this important Qur'anic passage that he had encountered. His generous response to this impromptu literary effort planted the seeds of confidence in me. I decided to compose a similar meditation on at least one passage from each of the 114 chapters of the Qur'an, every selection touching some unique aspect of Islamic revelation. I decided to retain the order of these selected passages as they appear in the Holy Qur'an rather than to arrange them under any thematic system of classification. In this way I hoped to suggest the atmosphere and even the esoteric significance of the Arabic text. This book is not an explanation of the Qur'an but an invocation of the Qur'an.

Most of the selections consist of only a few verses, highly condensed in the original Arabic and liberally expanded upon in my meditations. Working from the various English translations available, I attempted to stay close to the basic meaning of the text while further unfolding some of the beauty and profundity of the original. I composed a title for each selection, treating it not as a mere fragment, but as an integral whole.

As I continued to work, certain linguistic structures developed, such as the phrase "My beloved Muhammad," which does not occur in the Arabic but which I introduce as a reminder that the entire Holy Qur'an consists of the words of Allah addressed tenderly and lovingly to His Prophet Muhammad, and through him, to humanity as a whole.

For those passages in which God directly addresses humanity through the voice of the Prophet, I have introduced phrases such as "My dear human beings who desire to become fully human," again dramatizing the fact that it is always Allah who is speaking in the Qur'an, never the Prophet of Allah. At those points in the text where Allah speaks reflexively, and which are usually rendered into English as "We create" or "We protect," I have introduced phrases such as "the Ultimate Source now speaking creates" or "the Source of Power now speaking protects," in order to suggest the intimate sense of hearing the original Divine Communication. The Qur'an is the mysterious voice of Allah, not a book of sacred history or theology. I have developed various English synonyms for the Arabic Name *Allah*, such *as Ultimate Source, Ever-Present Source, Source of Being, Source of Power, Source of Love, Source of Life,* and *Source of Light.* This reflects the plurality of Divine Names in the original. Of course, I use the term *Allah* very often, choosing not to translate it as *God,* in order to encourage English speakers to become sensitive to the term *Allah* as used by many millions of people on the planet today. To dramatize the fact that Allah the Most High is not some local deity in cultural or religious competition with other deities, I occasionally use a phrase such as "the Ultimate Source, Who calls Itself by countless Divine Names."

From this metaphor of Allah as the Source, there developed variations on the phrases "turning toward the Source" and "those who affirm the Source" to express experientially the Arabic terms for *belief* and *believer,* which are not doctrinal terms, but existential ones. Similarly, variations of the phrases "turning away from the Source" and "those who negate the Source" cover the Arabic terms for *unbelief* and *unbeliever.* Many such English expressions have developed during the ten years I have worked on this manuscript. They are used to suggest the grandeur of expression and the profundity of meaning that cannot be contained in any literal translation of the highly condensed Arabic original, which often amounts to a kind of sacred shorthand.

I have also introduced into these meditations various connecting links—for instance, in the biblical stories narrated by the Holy Qur'an—links that are not expressly stated in the Arabic. I have done this to retain in English the fluency and dramatic quality of the original. The Holy Qur'an not only dispenses with narrative links, but also leaves certain important elements of spiritual practice and mystical lore to be implied rather than stated. Some of these teachings I have made more explicit.

Certain scholars may object that the many refinements in contemplative discipline and esoteric wisdom found in the later mystical tradition of Islam—sometimes called Sufism—are not actually alluded to in the original text of the Qur'an. But traditional devout Muslim practitioners do indeed find this richness of mystical meaning in the Holy Qur'an, building on centuries of inspired exegesis and deep contemplative experience. My attempt in these meditations is to dramatize what, from my own experience in the world of Islam, the sensitive Muslim person actually feels when reading the Holy Qur'an or listening raptly, sometimes without clear verbal comprehension, to the melodious chanting of the classical Arabic.

Concerning the various levels of meaning that are encountered by devout Muslims in their Book of Books, I should stress that my meditations stay very close to the basic level of meaning in the Holy Qur'an. For this fundamental stratum of significance I would not use the phrase "literal meaning," because this suggests some sort of *merely literal* meaning, which can be dismissed as relatively unimportant in relation to the high mystical quest. Nothing could be farther from the way the committed Muslim regards this precious book of revelation. What I would call the "basic meaning" of the verses is profoundly important. It forms the *basis* of Muslim practice and experiential belief, without which the various higher levels of mystical meaning would be nullified.

Occasionally my renderings of certain Qur'anic themes, such as the mercifully purifying nature of hellfire, begin to enter the range of intermediate mystical meaning. This intermediate range is also entered in my meditation on the enlightenment of the Prophet Abraham, an interpretation of the Qur'anic text that was confirmed by Sheikh Muzaffer.

Hardly ever do I enter the highest levels of esoteric teaching concealed in the Holy Qur'an, because they are largely unknown to me and are not contained in books, but are passed intimately from teacher to student in the intricate, sacred world of the contemplative Orders of Islam. Sheikh Muzaffer has explained that nowhere in his extensive published works does he discuss any teaching higher than the intermediate level, for he considers that the highest mystical teachings should be conveyed only to individuals at the proper moment in their own spiritual development. An esoteric truth that is misunderstood or misused can create serious obstacles to authentic contemplative life, as well as inject false images into the general cultural understanding of the mystical quest.

Consider one example of basic meaning and intermediate meaning in the Holy Qur'an. There are four rivers in Paradise: of water, milk, wine, and honey. The basic meaning is that in the realm of afterdeath experience, the soul progressively encounters these four levels of blessing, each more intensely concentrated than the last. To add that the contemplative, or mystic, can taste these rivers of spiritual experience while still living on earth is beginning to touch the intermediate level of meaning.

However, as Sheikh Muzaffer informed me, the esoteric

tradition of Islam teaches that these four rivers of Paradise refer as well to subtle nerve channels in the human body, which the practitioner is instructed by the Sheikh to activate in various ways. Now we are truly encountering the higher levels of meaning, which refer to an esoteric science passed down through the generations by the sheikhs of the mystical Orders of Islam.

I cannot comment in detail concerning levels of meaning even higher than this, because such principles are known only to the spiritual adepts. One might say that the secret of mystical union is at issue here. The ecstatic lover who disappears totally into the Divine Love emerges again as an intimate friend of Allah, with a human body composed solely of love. Such beings alone can truly understand the depth of the Holy Qur'an. As Sheikh Muzaffer once remarked, such adepts can find in the Qur'anic verses clear predictions of even the most ordinary events that will occur to them during the course of the day.

To return to our original example, my Sheikh stressed that the soul will indeed encounter these four rivers upon entering Paradise, and will undergo the subtle levels of experience that the rivers symbolize. This is the basic level of meaning that is never to be dispensed with. This description of Paradise is not a mere metaphor expressing spiritual possibilities for the human being here on earth. Sheikh Muzaffer made clear that both of these levels of meaning—the afterdeath experiences and the esoteric spiritual practices—are entirely objective and mutually complementary.

I do not want to leave the impression that Qur'anic teaching exists on some "remote" mystical level. Much of the most powerful spiritual instruction of the Holy Qur'an centers around such immediately accessible themes as selfless compassion, commitment to justice, faithfulness to moral standards and daily spiritual disciplines, tenderness toward all creatures, and deep gratitude to the Source of Creation. These Qur'anic themes, although they, too, are elaborated on higher and higher levels of meaning, appeal directly to every human being who wishes to be fully human. The contemplative life and the ethical life are never actually separable. Both the longing for mystic return into the ultimate Source and the commitment to offer kindness and justice to all beings on earth are taught by the Holy Qur'an as essential aspects of a complete human life. Every person who truly walks the exalted way of Islam is seeking immersion in the mystery of Allah the Most High, and is also deeply engaged in the daily life and welfare of the human family.

PART TWO

Meditations on the
Holy Qur'an

Chapter Four

REALITY

Allah: The Ground of Being

T he *Allah* of the Qur'an is not a thought form, a "god" among other gods, or, in the strictest sense a "personal God" at all. If we look at the Arabic word AL-LAH, we find it composed of two roots, one that affirms existence *(AL)*, the other than denies it *(LA)*. This *yes* and *no* of existence, held in balance, points toward a reality that we can approximately translate as "Oneness" or the "Ground of Being." This root understanding forms the basis of the Muslim confession of faith, called the *shahada*, which means the "experiencing" that "there is no Reality except the One Reality" (in Arabic *la ilaha illa'llah*). Saying this phrase is all that is needed to make one a *Muslim* in name. Actually experiencing it, and living according to this experience in one's dealings with others, makes one a *Muslim* in reality, that is, a person surrendered to the ground of Being, *Allah.*

Where Hixon's translation that follows refers to misplaced trust in "elemental forces," a contemporary reader might substitute the words "forces of rampant materialism" in order to hear the radical sense that Muhammad's original listeners would have experienced.

The first sura of the Qur'an, *Fateha,* translated here in full as "The Direct Path," holds the entire essence of the Qur'an within it, according to some Muslim traditions. Muslims recite it as part of their prayers five times a day. Another passage they often recite with it is Sura 112, the last in this section, translated here by Hixon as "The Only One." It contains another profound celebration of the nature of Unity and Reality.

—Ed.

✂

The Direct Path

My beloved Muhammad, please inspire My precious human beings to affirm with their entire being the Majestic Name, Allah Most High, Who is the Ultimate Source now speaking through you as tender Mercy and sublime Love. Please teach humanity to pray this way:

"Spontaneous praise arising from the hearts and minds of all beings flows toward Allah alone, the Ever-Present Source and Goal of Being, Who sustains and cherishes every being, the Source of Love, Who overflows constantly with compassion and forgiveness. The Supreme Source draws all conscious beings to their Day of Truth, their homecoming into the Radiance of Allah. To Allah alone, as the Source of Being, can living beings truly offer their entire being. From Allah alone, as the Source of Power and Love, can true strength and guidance be received. Most precious Allah, You alone teach human beings to turn consciously toward their own True Source. This is the direct path of Islam, revealed through all the Prophets and courageously taken by the lovers of Love who follow the Call of Love directly to the Source of Love. This is not one of the mundane paths that wander through

Creation, taken by those who heedlessly turn away from the Source of Creation."

—Meditation on *Holy Qur'an* 1:1–7

❧

The Original Source

My cherished human beings who long to become truly human, turn your lives toward Allah alone, the Source of Power, Who emanates you and all the beings that ever existed before you. This conscious turning toward your own True Source is the way to learn purity of heart and compassionate action. Turn ceaselessly toward Allah Most High, Whose Power presents you this green and blue planet as a resting place and this brilliant tent of stars as a seat of inspiration, Whose Mercy descends as sweet rain to create the earthly fruits you need for sustenance. Never resort to magic or cosmic forces you instinctively know to be secondary, but rely for spiritual strength on the Original Source alone.

If you doubt the authenticity of these Divine Words spoken by the Ultimate Source through My devoted servant Muhammad, then try to compose words like them and find impartial witnesses who will confirm your words to be of equal value. You will certainly not succeed. If you continue to deny that the Source of Wisdom communicates directly with humanity through the Prophets, allowing such negation to grow deep within you, then during the sleep of death Divine Splendor must appear as consuming fire to burn your negativity away.

My beloved Messenger, please bring joyous news to those whose whole lives affirm Love through constant compassion and purity of heart, that they will awaken immediately from the sleep of death into the direct Presence of Allah, experienced as

mystical gardens of Paradise that flow with rivers of peace. The
fruits of earthly life are then understood to be reflections of the
fruits of Paradise. The delight known here between friends and
lovers will there be brought to perfect purity and fullness. There
the ones who live for Love will live forever.

—Meditation on *Holy Qur'an* 2:21–5

∞

The Essence of Islam

There exists only one Supreme Source, one inexhaustible Power
calling Itself Allah, the profoundly living One, the Life beyond
time that never diminishes. The One Reality never sleeps, nor
even for a moment rests Its embracing Awareness. To the One
alone belongs the emanation of planetary existence and the seven
higher planes of Being, as spreading rays of sunlight belong to a
single sun. There is no being who can turn toward the Ever-
Present Source in prayer or contemplation except through the
Power and Love that flow from the Source Itself. Since the Ultimate Source abides beyond time, It always remains perfectly aware
of what causes precede and what results follow from each event.
Human beings can comprehend nothing of this encompassing
Awareness save what Allah Most High transmits to them as gifts
of Grace. All Creation, including planetary and heavenly planes,
is the brilliant Throne of Allah. To sustain and protect this vast
manifestation of Divine Energy involves no effort at all for the
Original Source, Who is supremely transcendent and Who subsists solely as Radiance.

My beloved Muhammad, there should never be the slightest compulsion brought to bear upon any person to walk the exalted way of Islam. Allow humanity to be attracted spontaneously

to Islam by its utmost clarity, for Islam simply makes clear the truth that there can be only one Source. This truth dissolves the primal error that turns away from the Ultimate Source by mistaking various limited views to be ultimate. Whoever ceases to rely on any idol, on any limited human understanding, and relies for strength solely on the limitless Source, Who calls Itself Allah, has grasped the most trustworthy support, the clear and indestructible essence of Islam.

Allah Most Wise hears inwardly the spoken and unspoken prayers, and perceives intimately the open and hidden motivations of all beings. Allah Most Merciful gives the perfect guidance and full protection of His Divine Friendship to those who affirm the Source of Love with every breath. Those who live the life of constant spiritual affirmation, Allah Most High brings forth from the shadow realm of subjective impulses and limited concepts into the clear Light of the Source. But those who turn away from the Source of Light, who for guidance and protection rely on the graven images of limitation, are drawn from the clarity of Revelation into the realm of shadows, and will inevitably experience the Splendor of Allah as blinding fire.

—Meditation on *Holy Qur'an* 2:255–7

The Storm of Love

From the Source of Power, Who is now speaking, flash forth pure bolts of spiritual energy, the lightning of Allah that sparks fear in those whose lives express negation, and awakens luminous expectancy in those whose lives express affirmation. From the Source of Love, radiant clouds, heavy with the rain of Divine Compassion, are constantly emerging, and their awesome

thunder sings the deep praises of Allah Most High. Lost in wonder, angelic beings gaze from eternity upon this brilliant storm
of Love. The lightning of Allah can touch anyone instantly, chastening or quickening, and yet human beings still foolishly dispute
the existence of the Ever-Present Source.

Those who invoke Allah Most Merciful with intense prayer
feel immediately the unmistakable presence of the Living Truth,
whereas those who worship various elemental forces or etheric
beings do not experience the same flood of encompassing Holy
Presence. These misguided worshippers of Creation are like thirsty
wanderers who stretch forth their hands but cannot reach far
enough to touch the water in a deep well. The prayers of these
worshippers, who wander through Creation and who rely upon
Creation rather than turn toward the Source of Creation, cannot even moisten their dry lips. Yet all beings in the universe,
whether or not they consciously face their own True Source, are
bowing to Allah Most Sublime with their entire being through
every thought and action. Even their shadows, their secret ap-
prehensions and dark impulses, can exist only in relation to the
Source of Light.

—Meditation on *Holy Qur'an* 13:12–5

Magnificent Presence

Be assured that the Ultimate Source, Who is now speaking,
radiates and orchestrates every being and every event in perfect
harmony. The single Word of Power from the Source of Power
calls the totality of lives into Being more swiftly than the blink
of an eye.

Please remind your people, My beloved, that Allah Most High has allowed time to devastate countless nations. Urge them to contemplate history. Every action ever performed by human beings until the end of time, including each thought, significant or fleeting, is already inscribed in the Transcendent Qur'an, the encompassing Awareness of Allah.

Those who live in authentic awe of Allah will dwell always in His mysterious embrace, envisioned as boundless gardens of love beside eternal rivers of peace. From this level of ecstatic vision, souls will further ascend into the placeless abode of absolute certitude, the direct meeting and merging with the Living Truth, the magnificent Presence of the All-Powerful King.

—Meditation on *Holy Qur'an* 54:49–55

All-Encompassing Knowledge

Cherished humanity, please try to realize more vividly and directly what it means to assert that Allah Most High knows intimately every event occurring in the heavens and on earth. When three of you are talking together privately, Allah is actually present as if He were a fourth member of the conversation. If five of you are gathered in close consultation, Allah is like a sixth, silently seeing every gesture and hearing every word. Whether fewer than that or more, Allah Most Wise is immediately present with human beings, whatever the conditions may be. On the Day of Truth, souls should not be surprised to hear the All-Merciful One recounting, with absolute precision, each thought and action of their entire lifetimes. This is what it truly means to affirm that Allah is All-Encompassing Knowledge.

—Meditation on *Holy Qur'an* 58:7

⬦

Allah Is Allah

My beloved Muhammad, if the Supreme Source, Who is now speaking, sent this Holy Qur'an down upon a giant mountain rather than into the indestructible diamond of your secret soul, the mountain would be obliterated and leveled into dust by the awesome impact of Divine Power and the unbearable weight of Divine Meaning. These metaphors are revealed through you by the Source of Wisdom, that humanity may learn to contemplate the awesomeness of Allah Most High, His Prophet, and His Holy Qur'an.

Allah alone is Allah. There is no reality apart from Ultimate Reality. Allah alone is the Perfect Knower of all visible structures and invisible principles. Allah alone is infinite Mercy and unconditional Love.

Allah alone is Allah. There is no reality apart from Ultimate Reality. Allah alone is the Mystical King: All-Holy, All-Peaceful, All-Trustworthy, All-Protecting, All-Powerful, All-Encompassing, All-Sublime. The radiant beauty of Being streams solely from Allah Most High, Who is beyond every possible human conception or description.

Allah alone is Allah, the formless Source, Who emanates and evolves all the intricate forms of Creation. Allah alone is manifest through the Divine Beauty of His ninety-nine mystical Names. The very nature and function of both eternal heavenly being and temporal earthly existence is to praise Allah, Who is boundless Power and complete Wisdom.

—Meditation on *Holy Qur'an* 59:21–4

The Kingdom of Reality

The infinite fountain of blessing is Allah Most High, Whose embrace of Power and Love constitutes the entire Kingdom of Reality. The Single Source behind all beings and events projects this vast drama of life and death as an education for souls, who learn to express the beautiful Attributes of Allah through contemplation and action within the realm of temporality. Allah Most High is awesome Power as well as tender Mercy and absolute Forgiveness. The ascending planes of Being and levels of awareness are luminous reflections of Divine Power, harmoniously interwoven with Divine Compassion, to create the perfect environment for training souls.

Those whose whole being is oriented toward the Source and Goal of Being do not perceive the slightest imperfection or injustice in the boundless kingdom of the All-Merciful One. Look deeply into this radiant Creation of realms and planes, My beloved. Can you observe the slightest fragmentation or disharmony anywhere? Contemplate this Kingdom of Reality again and again. The gaze of your spiritual understanding, returning to you weary and dazzled, will then come to rest in the Source of Perfection.

—Meditation on *Holy Qur'an* 67:1–4

The Only One

My beloved Muhammad, please transmit these unique Words of Truth as the purest essence of Islam: "The One Reality, Who calls Itself Allah Most High, is peaceful Unity and harmonious

Completeness. This Supreme Oneness has not been generated by any power more primordial, nor has any being ever come into being independent of the Only One, Who is beyond time and eternity and Who is the Single Source and Goal of Being. There is nothing equal to the One and there is nothing beside the One, for apart from the One Reality, nothing is.

—Meditation on *Holy Qur'an* 112:1–4

COMMENTARY:
Creation: The Process of Becoming

A great deal of the Qur'an focuses on celebrations of cosmic beginnings. It does not view this Creation as a one-time event, however, but rather as an ongoing process. In this sense, the Qur'an expresses ideas compatible with spiritual views of evolution proposed by contemporary Jewish and Christian theologians. Like other *synchronic* languages, Arabic views the past as ongoing, receding into the horizon ahead of us, so to speak, as the future comes along behind us. The cosmic beginning of the caravan of Creation can include us at any moment that we sense our divine purpose in life opening up ahead of us. "The eternal Day of the Ever-Present Source is nearer to the human being than anyone can conceive—nearer than near, and even nearer than that" (Sura 75:34).

The Qur'an uses many different metaphors to point toward a reality that one can never fully describe, only experience. It also points to every element of Creation—every living being—as a symbol that can reveal this mystery to us. For this reason, nature itself expresses the divine reality and has been called by Muslim scholars "the Qur'an of Creation."

Islamic mystics and Sufis have long meditated upon Sura 24:35, the "verse of light," which is here translated by Lex Hixon as "Light." It provides another profound way of seeing ordinary reality in an extraordinary way. Likewise, Sura 38:71–85, translated here as "Primal Arrogance," describes the Qur'an's view of the origin of pride and self-centeredness. A similar story about Iblis's refusal to bow down to the First Human had already entered both early Jewish and Christian traditions by the time of Muhammad. The mystery of our individual self-awareness, in both its positive and negative aspects, preoccupied the Creation stories of all three traditions. "You are part of the mystery of My infinite Mercy," Allah says to Iblis here. First, however, we encounter Sura 2, which contains a section translated as "The Mystery of the Prophet Adam," an inner view of the familiar "Garden of Eden" story shared by the three Abrahamic traditions.

—Ed.

♃

The Mystery of the Prophet Adam

My beloved Muhammad, please transmit this profound Revelation to humanity: "My cherished ones, why do you close your eyes to the Power of the Ever-Present Source, Who is now speaking? The Power of Allah clothes you with organic life and will eventually remove this cloak, revealing an eternal garment of light for your return into Divine Light. The Power of Allah projects for your experience and spiritual evolution this entire planetary realm, and seven progressively more subtle heavenly realms. Allah is the encompassing Awareness, Who watches from within, each action and each thought on every plane of Being.

"Before time began, Allah Most High announced to the angels: 'Behold, I will create powerful and intelligent beings as My spiritual representatives and as the caretakers of planetary life.' Responding from the perspective of angelic vision, they asked, 'Most Exalted Allah, how can You evolve creatures there who will turn corrupt and wage war, while here we praise You as incorruptible?' Allah Most Sublime proclaimed: 'My Knowledge transcends yours utterly.'

"The Supreme Source taught the transcendental Adam the name of every being on every plane of Being, as well as the beautiful Mystical Names for the Source of Being. Revealing to the angels the entire spectrum of Creation, Allah then commanded: 'If you possess such penetrating vision, recite the names of My created beings.' The awestruck angels responded: 'All praise belongs to You and all knowledge is Yours alone, Most Precious Allah. We are conversant only with what You have taught us. You are embracing Awareness and complete Wisdom.' Then the heavenly Adam, empowered by the Source of Wisdom, recited for the angels the names of all beings. The Voice of Truth reminded the angels: 'Do you who express merely angelic intelligence forget that Allah knows the secrets of the planetary realm and the seven heavenly realms? Do you forget that Allah knows every thought, revealed or concealed? Bow with your entire being before the crown of My Creation, who mysteriously bears My Knowledge and My Essence.'

"So, before time began, the angels and other beings on the subtle planes bowed profoundly before the transcendental Adam, except for one etheric being named Iblis, who was intensely proud of his intelligence. Iblis became the first of those who arrogantly turn away from the Source of Being, who negate the very Ground of their own being, and who instinctively spread this negation in other minds and hearts. Iblis became the disintegrating force called Satan.

"The Voice of Truth then proclaimed: 'My beloved Adam, dwell with your wife in the primordial garden of Life and experience whatever you wish, except for the fruits that awaken sharp pangs of separation.' Adam consciously chose to ignore this admonition, through the mysterious Will of Allah that permitted the action of Satan, for the human soul wished to experience separation from the Source of Love and the consequent longing for Divine Love, cherished since by every traveler along the mystic path of return. Thus the human soul was drawn down from the bliss of transcendental Life into the struggle of time.

"The Voice of Truth proclaimed to Adam and to all souls: 'You must descend into temporality to experience separation and conflict. Remain for a lifetime in the school of longing, where you will encounter mere reflections of the delight that is above time!' Yet Allah Most Merciful turned lovingly toward the temporal Adam, granting him illumination and opening him as a channel for the Divine Revelation. My beloved Adam became the first Prophet, the first messenger in time sent from the Eternal Source. Allah spontaneously turns and floods the hearts and minds of human beings with radiance, for Allah is tender Mercy and sublime Love.

"At the beginning of history, the Voice of Truth decreed: 'My cherished human souls, descend among the veils of separation. You will receive My Guidance there, and those who respond wholeheartedly to the Revelation flowing through the noble Adam and through the pure stream of Prophets to come will never be overwhelmed by fear or sorrow and will return directly to the Ultimate Source. But the souls who turn away from the Source of Love, rejecting the demonstrations of Love that flow through My noble Messengers, will need to experience their return into the beautiful Light of Eternity as the plunge into purifying fire.'"

—Meditation on *Holy Qur'an* 2:28–39

⌘

The Throne of Manifestation

During six primal and measureless days of Power, the Supreme Source radiated the luminous structure of the planetary realm and the seven heavenly realms as tangible and intangible planes of Being. The Source of Being, Who is now speaking, is mystically established upon this vast Throne of Manifestation. The full Divine Presence can therefore be subtly experienced throughout Creation, from the simple rhythm of day and night to the cosmic symphony of stars, as all events flow harmoniously from the Source of Harmony. The entire Creation, coherently and justly governed, emanates from the One, Who cherishes and sustains all realms and planes of Being, the Source of Holiness that calls Itself by countless beautiful names.

My beloved Muhammad, please instruct humanity to turn inwardly toward the mystery of Allah, to pray humbly within the secret heart, for no one can turn completely toward the Source of Love without the training of inwardness.

Please warn human beings that by succumbing to impulses of aggression or greed they bring themselves into disharmony with the very principles of justice and compassion by which Allah Most High establishes and governs the Creation. A life of disharmony closes the inner channel of the heart to the ever-flowing Source of Love.

Please demonstrate clearly to human beings how to turn toward their own True Source through daily prayer, immersing themselves in profound awe and intense longing. Allah's tender Mercy streams abundantly to all humanity through those whose whole lives affirm Love.

—Meditation on *Holy Qur'an* 7:54–6

The Rain of Life

Contemplate life as fresh rain showered abundantly on receptive ground from the Ever-Present Source, Who is like the vast sky. This pure rainwater, mingling with the earth, causes the boundless variety of seeds to sprout and flourish, providing ample nourishment for all creatures. Imagine the spiritual blindness of those who deny the existence of the Original Source, the very sky from which life-giving water descends, and who insist that they alone have power over the fertile expanse of this earth, turned fruitful and beautiful by the rain of life. With terrible suddenness, during night or day, a ray of light like fire can radiate from the Source of Power and reduce rich orchards and pastures to fields of straw, without leaving a trace of the abundance experienced only moments before. For those who meditate deeply, this parable from the Source of Wisdom presents a clear teaching to rely upon the Ultimate Source alone. Thus the Voice of Allah invites human beings home into Divine Peace and guides them along the Direct Path of surrender. These souls return to the Single Source, along the noble way that is called *Islam*.

—Meditation on *Holy Qur'an* 10:24–5

The Arrogant Ones

Allah alone radiates the entire spectrum of heaven and earth during six original days of Power. His Throne is the flow of Divine Energy behind the manifest universe, and His entire Creation exists simply as testing and teaching for the soul.

My beloved Muhammad, when you give assurance to humanity that after the sleep of death they will awaken into the Direct Presence of Allah, those who live in negation of Love will respond: "This awakening again after dying is just a sorcerer's dream." When the Source of Power does not immediately chasten these arrogant ones, but allows them gradually to create their own suffering, they mock: "If Allah actually exists, how can we continue to deny Him without the slightest adverse consequence?" Yet when the Day of Truth dawns for them, they will be unable to avoid any of the consequences of their thoughts and actions, being utterly exposed and permeated by the burning light of the Living Truth, which they had mocked.

When the Source of Love pours sweet forgiveness into the souls and generous abundance into the earthly lives of such arrogant ones, their hearts begin to turn toward Allah Most High, but when sweetness and abundance are withdrawn even slightly to discipline them in spiritual commitment, these rebellious ones return to negation and their fleeting gratitude evaporates. When the Source of Delight allows such persons to taste joy instead of the suffering created by their own negativity, arrogance arises once more and they exclaim: "Now our troubles are gone forever." Thus do the arrogant separate themselves from the Source of Love. Compare them, My beloved, with those who patiently and humbly accept all events as gifts and teachings from Allah Most High, and whose every act, including even each breath, expresses selfless compassion and purity of heart. These sublime lovers of Love inwardly experience nothing except the fragrance and sweetness of My Forgiveness, and eventually they will receive in full My vast treasure of Love.

—Meditation on *Holy Qur'an* 11:7–11

The Green Tapestry

The Supreme Source, Who is now speaking, radiates vast systems of stars that glow like bright palaces scattered throughout the cosmos as a reminder, for those who can contemplate them truly, of the Beauty and Power of Allah. With the sublime principle of unity, the Single Source has protected this universe against the disintegrating forces sparked by the cosmic rebel, Satan. Through human beings, these negative forces have entered Allah's pristine Creation, but they are constantly pursued and driven from the precious human heart by the bright flame of Truth.

As a living stage for this drama of purification, the Source of Power unfolds the delicate green tapestry of Earth, anchoring it with primordial mountains. The Source of Life evolves innumerable forms of organic life, each in precise balance with the others, providing perfectly for the sustenance of human beings and every other being as well. But this earthly storehouse of abundance cannot flourish apart from the Source of Life, Who emanates with harmony and precision all the fruitful powers of life. From the Living Source alone emerge seed-bearing winds, life-giving rains, and thirst-quenching springs. Human beings do not own or control these natural treasures, for the Source of Life alone gives and withdraws life. All manifest Being belongs solely to the Source and Goal of Being, Allah Most High, Who knows which persons truly aspire and which merely conspire and Who will eventually draw every soul home into the radiance that is embracing Awareness and complete Wisdom.

—Meditation on *Holy Qur'an* 15:16–25

Creation

My beloved Muhammad, please remind those who question the existence of the Supreme Source to contemplate My Creation most intensely. Teach them to envision the universe in its original state as an expanse of light without borders or limits, which the Source of Power gradually shapes into life-bearing worlds. Then invite the soul to contemplate the Source of Life continuously pouring forth the Water of Life as countless streams of living beings. Meditating thus, fundamental doubts will disappear.

Instruct humanity to concentrate on the Source of Power establishing primordial mountains to give the earth stability, opening steep ravines and broad valleys through these mountains as paths and dwelling places for living creatures, as the Source of Life gracefully envelops the planet with a life-protecting dome of atmosphere. Gazing at this process of Creation with eyes of true understanding, how can anyone fail to see manifest Being as one vast demonstration of Love? Yet many still turn away from the Source of Love.

This entire Creation radiates from Allah alone, Who establishes its dynamic harmony, which is revealed even by the simple rhythm of day and night, as the sun, moon, and stars stream brilliantly through one encompassing sky.

—Meditation on *Holy Qur'an* 21:30–3

Light

Calling Itself Allah, the Supreme Source is the One Light illuminating every heavenly and earthly realm. My beloved Muhammad, please transmit this profound meditation. The Light of Allah is the window that opens beyond all Creation. On the sill of this shining window rests the precious lamp of the human soul, whose flame is pure and steady, protected by the transparent crystal of the heart that glistens delicately, like a star, with the soul's light. This lamp, ignited by Divine Love alone, burns aromatic oil from the Tree of Life, that transcendent Tree found nowhere on earth, neither in the East nor in the West. This fragrant oil of wisdom radiates illumination spontaneously, not needing to be touched by any earthly fire. Thus the light of the soul and Source of Light behind it blend, merge, and reappear in the mystery of eternal companionship, as the Light of Allah within the Light of Allah.

Speaking thus to humanity through the most subtle figurative language, the Source of Wisdom guides to enlightenment whomever It wills, for Allah is the One encompassing Awareness.

—Meditation on *Holy Qur'an* 24:35

Living Parables

My beloved Muhammad, please teach humanity to observe that whatever lives in this planetary realm spontaneously celebrates the Source of Life. The birds, simply by spreading their wings for flight, are praising Allah Most High, Who knows intimately the instinctive prayer and praise expressed through the most minute action of every being. From Allah alone radiates the great affirmation that is Heaven and Earth, and to Allah alone, the Source and Goal of Being, is this entire kingdom of Being returning home.

Please instruct humanity to understand as a living parable how, through the Power of Allah, the wind gathers clouds and merges them, and how from this union life-giving rain showers forth as an essential blessing for the earth. Contemplate how there emerge from the Source of Power thunderheads like massive mountains from which fierce storms sweep into the valleys of human life, chastening those whom Allah Most Wise wishes to chasten, and turning aside from those whom Allah Most Merciful wishes to protect. The dynamic flash of lightning that profoundly startles human vision as well as the harmonious rhythm of day and night both spring from the Source of Power. Deep spiritual teaching is contained for those who can read the living parables of Allah Most High. Every creature that flows as Water of Life from the Source of Life is a parable, spoken by the cosmic Qur'an, which teaches humanity to gaze with eyes of wisdom upon all My Creations: aquatic creatures, reptiles, and four-footed and two-footed creatures. Whatever is willed by the Source of Being comes spontaneously into Being and bears profound meaning. Allah Most Sublime is the Single Source of all the fruitful forces that function as this universe.

—Meditation on *Holy Qur'an* 24:41–5

❧

Demonstrations of Power and Love

Among the demonstrations of Power that flow continuously from the Source of Power is the Creation of the marvelous human organism simply from substances of the earth. Consider how many of these precious human forms are scattered across the entire planet.

Among the demonstrations of Love that flow continuously from the Source of Love is the Creation for every human being of an intimately related partner in life, providing communion, strength, and repose. Allah Most High has established between wife and husband the possibility for truly selfless compassion and profound love. The relationship of marriage contains deep spiritual teaching for those who contemplate deeply.

Among the demonstrations of Power that flow continuously from the Source of Power is the Creation of Being itself as a subtle structure of heavenly and earthly planes containing an inexhaustible variety of languages and life forms. The entire realm of life becomes profound spiritual teaching for those who contemplate profoundly.

Among the demonstrations of Love that flow continuously from the Source of Love is the peaceful sleep by which beings are refreshed at night or during the day. Thus the natural activities of daily existence, all the ways that conscious beings instinctively and intuitively reach out for the gracious and abundant gifts of Allah, become clear spiritual teaching for those who perceive clearly.

Among the demonstrations of Power that flow continuously from the Source of Power are lightning bolts that fall from the stormy sky, awakening awe of Allah Most High and the expectation of life-giving rain. The pure rainwater, which, through the Blessing of Allah, showers so abundantly upon this earth, bringing what is dry and withered back to life, presents signs of Revelation and Resurrection into Paradise to those who meditate truly.

Among the demonstrations of Love that flow continuously from the Source of Love is that the entire universe remains poised, waiting for the Call of Allah, ready to return into its Original Source. When the mystic Call of the Ever-Present Source is heard by human beings, they emerge gloriously from the veils of limitation into the limitless Radiance of Allah.

—Meditation on *Holy Qur'an* 30:20–5

∝

Resurrection

My noble Messenger, please remind human beings that the Source of Power generates their organic existence in the womb from the most minute drop of earthly substance. Forgetting this humble beginning and their total dependence on the Source of Power, they become so blinded by self-importance that they come into open conflict with Allah Most High, or even reject entirely the sovereignty of the Ultimate Source. Elevating their own limited concepts, and worshipping them instead of Allah, such persons lose touch with the intuitive understanding that their very being originates only from the Source of Being. Those who actively deny their own True Source are gradually permeated by aggressive negation. Concerning the higher manifestation of the human form in Paradise, they will remark with irony: "Are bones which have become dust beneath the earth going to function again?" My beloved, enlighten such darkened minds with My Divine Words: "The body in Paradise will emanate from the

same Source of Light that has projected this earthly body, and
that consciously radiates all the vast realms and levels of Creation. Consider how from a green tree the Source of Power brings
forth golden flame after the wood is cut and kindled. So is the
green tree of the earthly body, through the Power of the All-
Merciful One, transformed into the luminous body that dwells
in Paradise."

Urge people to consider whether the Supreme Source, Who
dearly emanates the entire planetary realm, is not able to emanate higher planes of Being as well. They will realize intuitively
that this must be possible for Allah, Who simply by following all
beings, creates all beings. Whatever Allah Most High wishes to
manifest He calls into existence by the primordial command:
"Be!" The brightness of Being shines from Allah alone. His Hand
of Merciful Power shapes every event, and the very nature of
Creation is to praise and to return into the Source of Creation.

—Meditation on *Holy Qur'an* 36:77–83

∾

Primal Arrogance

The Ultimate Source, Who is now speaking, proclaimed before
time to the vast circle of heavenly beings: "Gaze upon the mystery of Divine Power. I will now evolve from mere clay a living
being who will be the crown of My entire Creation. When I
have shaped humanity most intricately, breathing into it My Own
Life as its soul, you must all prostrate prayerfully before this
unique vessel of My Living Spirit." When this supreme mystery
of Divine Manifestation was accomplished, countless ranks of
angels and lesser heavenly beings bowed in graceful unison—
all except the etheric Iblis, who was the first being to become

infected with pride and to exist in the mode of negation.

For the spiritual instruction of all conscious beings, Allah Most High inquired: "Iblis, what strange impulse has prevented you from offering reverence to the most remarkable of all Creations, the only being whom I have touched and shaped directly with My Own Hands of Love and Power?" The one blinded by arrogance responded: "You evolved my exalted form from etheric energy and this human form from mere earthly substance. I am more refined and cannot bow before what is less refined." Allah Most High declared: "You have decisively turned away from the Source of Wisdom and have become infused with your own negativity, which will cling to you until the Terrible Purification." Iblis demanded: "Allow me to operate freely until the Day of Judgment dawns." Allah Most Wise then decreed: "Iblis will exist until the end of time."

Intoxicated with pride, primal arrogance then proclaimed to the exalted Creator: "Through the subtle intelligence that I have received from You, I will draw human beings away from their own True Source into the constant service of their limited selves. Only Your most dedicated lovers will escape my wiles." The Source of Wisdom responded to Iblis: "You are part of the mystery of My infinite Mercy. You will lead countless human beings along the way of return through the purifying Fire of Hell. These are your arrogant followers who could never gently and humbly walk along My Path of Surrender. But all souls will return only to Me."

—Meditation on *Holy Qur'an* 38:71–85

✑

Six Mysterious Days of Power

My noble Messenger, those who doubt the existence of the Ever-Present Source now speaking through you should be answered with these Words of Truth: "How can you question the Source of Power, Who shapes this entire universe in the first two mysterious Days of Power, when you accept without question the existence of the limited cosmic forces that you investigate and revere? Please enter sincerely into the contemplation of Allah Most High, Who is the Single Source of Being. Allah alone establishes the primordial mountains of manifestation and blesses the broad earth of evolving life with fruitfulness. During the second two mysterious Days of Power, the Source of Power harmoniously evolves the diverse forms of living creatures and whatever environments of sustenance and protection they may need.

"After these four primal Days of Power, Allah Most High concentrates His Presence within the sphere of Being, which is composed of etheric substance like clear vapor, and calls into the hearts of all beings within all realms of Being: 'Do you wish to surrender your individual will consciously and return together with supreme joy into your True Source, or shall you be drawn back by Allah without knowing?' All souls in the pretemporal Universe of Souls respond spontaneously: 'Most precious Allah, we long to travel knowingly along the mystic way of return.'

"So during the final two mysterious Days of Power, the Source of Power creates seven progressively more subtle planes of existence and consciousness, revealing on each plane a new level of love and knowledge for the souls who will return along this path of mystical ascension into the Source of Peace.

"The Source of Power scatters stars as countless lamps of light and life throughout cosmic space, which is but the reflection of the lowest and least subtle of the seven heavens and which is a reservoir of energy for the preservation of the earthly plane of Being. This is the vast drama of Creation and Return as decreed by the boundless Power and encompassing Wisdom of Allah."

—Meditation on *Holy Qur'an* 41:9–12

Divine Creativity

The hearts and minds of all beings share a common sense for the Source of Being. Were someone to be asked suddenly, "Who creates the heavens and the earth?" Such a person would instinctively respond: "Some Supreme Power and Intelligence must be the Source of this universe." So, My beloved, please teach persons to explore their own intuitive sense of the Divine Creativity. Give them spiritual instruction to contemplate the Source of Love preparing the earth for humanity as carefully as a mother prepares a cradle for her infant. Tell them to envision valleys and rivers as ways established by the Source of Power for beings to travel and be guided across this vast planet. Encourage them to meditate on the sweet rain, which soaks the earth at the proper season as the Source of Life reviving land that appears dead, and as a living parable for the eternal awakening of the soul from its sleep of death. Ask them as well to observe Allah's subtle and continuous Creation of every form of life through the perfect harmony of male and female principles.

Teach clearly that Allah alone makes possible for human beings the use of ships and steeds. When traveling swiftly on various vehicles, My servants should remember that they are partaking of the marvelous blessings that radiate constantly from the single Source. They should call out prayerfully in the midst of their exhilaration: "All glory and praise to the Source of Power and Wisdom, Who alone makes possible what we accomplish. May our hearts turn ceaselessly in joyous gratitude toward the Ultimate Source of the Universe, the Source of Love to Whom the souls of Love are ecstatically returning."

—Meditation on *Holy Qur'an* 43:9–14

Life Blood

Are those who doubt the existence of the realm beyond death foolish enough to think that the boundless Source of Power becomes weary while creating and sustaining the physical universe? No, even they are not that foolish. But if they can accept My spontaneous and effortless Creation of the physical plane of Being, why are they so uncertain about My consummate spiritual Creation called Paradise?

The Ultimate Source emanates the human soul simultaneously on both physical and spiritual planes of Being. The Ever-Present Source knows what doubts the soul whispers secretly to itself here on earth, for the Source of Life is nearer to the human being than the very life blood that courses through the body's central vein.

—Meditation on *Holy Qur'an* 50:15–6

❦

Infinitely More

My servants who respond to the Divine Promise with devoted hearts, and who therefore live in constant inward awe of the All-Merciful One, will be drawn deep into what appear as radiant gardens, and will hear the Voice of Allah: "Come. Enter My Being in perfect peace. This is the eternal Day." The souls mystically entering the Source of Love will receive whatever spiritual experience they desire. Within the Ultimate Source there is infinitely more than any soul can desire.

—Meditation on *Holy Qur'an* 50:31–5

❦

The Spiritual Dimension

Those who live in complete awe of Allah Most High will be purified and will experience directly what can be indicated only indirectly as eternal gardens and radiant fountains, for the gifts they will receive from the Source of Love are beyond description. These surrendered souls are rigorously prepared for this overwhelming direct encounter with Divine Splendor by earthly lives of sheer goodness, expressed through constant small acts of tenderness and kindness toward all beings. Immersed in the delight of prayer, those who already belong to Paradise sleep only a few hours each night and rise again before dawn to ask forgiveness for the slightest lapse in their remembrance of the Ever-Present Source. Whatever abundance these intimate friends of Allah receive from the Source of Abundance is always shared with those who ask for help, as well as with those who do not ask.

Wherever one looks in this universe are signs of Divine Presence for those who are consciously aligned with the Ultimate Source of the Universe. Most intimately are these signs to be discerned by human beings within themselves, although many persons fail to perceive the spiritual dimension of their own awareness. My beloved one, please teach humanity to seek nourishment and delight from pure consciousness, and to look deep into themselves to discover the eternal life promised by the Source of Life. That human awareness is spiritual in nature and can therefore commune directly with Allah Most High is just as certain as the fact that human beings can express meaning and thereby understand each other. The very Source of heaven and earth, Who is now speaking, stands as solemn witness that these are Words of Truth.

—Meditation on *Holy Qur'an* 51:15–23

⋘⋙

Nearer than Near

The eternal Day of the Ever-Present Source is nearer to the human being than anyone can conceive—nearer than near, and even nearer than that. How else could it be? Do people really imagine that souls are far from Allah Most High, left by the Divine Mercy to wander aimlessly?

The precious human body emerges when a mere drop of potency is received into a fertile receptacle of blood. It then evolves intricately, by the mysterious permission of Allah, assuming male or female form. The two genders and their union exist to reflect the Divine Attributes of Completeness and Harmony. Perceiving this wondrous Creation of the material body, how can the intelligence of humanity doubt that the Source of Power can recreate human beings after death on immaterial planes of existence?

—Meditation on *Holy Qur'an* 75:34–40

Spiritual Gardens

Has not the Source of Love, Who is now speaking, prepared with tender care the vast expanse of this earth as a dwelling place for living beings? Has not the Source of Power anchored this spacious and fertile realm with giant mountains?

The Source of Life evolves living beings in balanced pairs, male and female, the express the Divine Completeness. The Source of Wisdom designs both refreshing sleep in the darkness of night, that cool garment for body and mind, and exhilarating action during the brightness of the day.

The Source of Being emanates as immaterial spheres seven planes of existence above this planetary plane, and has generated in the physical space below these heavenly realms the blazing lamp of the sun as light for the external eyes.

My beloved one, pointedly ask your people: "Does the Source of Abundance ever fail to send down upon the planet and upon the receptive human soul cascades of life-giving rain? Is this not why the vast variety of grains, fruits, and greens spring forth outwardly, and why spiritual gardens of surpassing beauty are inwardly blossoming?"

—Meditation on *Holy Qur'an* 78:6–16

Nourishment

My beloved Muhammad, please ask humanity to contemplate how beings are nourished by the fruits of the earth as a living parable for how souls are sustained by Allah Most High.

The Source of Life pours forth abundant rain upon the planetary realm, shaped and made fertile by the Source of Power. A vast profusion of natural growth springs forth from every kind of soil: fields of grain, grapevines and tender greens, olive trees on the mountainside, and date palms in the desert. As intense blessing from the Source of Love, human beings grow irrigated gardens, dense with shade trees, and orchards of sweet fruit. By the Power and Permission of Allah, the oasis of human existence is surrounded by rich pasture land, a green expanse where animals graze, and which is soothing to the eyes.

—Meditation on *Holy Qur'an* 80:24–32

Angelic Protectors

Cherished humanity, what has veiled from the eyes of your understanding the boundless generosity of Allah Most High? The Source of Power emanates you eternally as souls, and creates you temporally as living creatures subtly evolved to express perfect harmony. The Source of Love composes your being as a pure forms of His Own Love. Yet somehow you disregard the sublime gifts you have received, and you ignore as well the onrushing Day of Truth by dismissing the warning of My Holy Qur'an as myth or imagination. You must come to know with absolute

certitude that from above your conscious being, as stars above
the earth, there gaze angelic protectors, noble and impassive.
Upon pages of light in the invisible book of your life, which will
become visible on the Day of Truth, these heavenly beings record
all your actions and reactions. Even the most secret motivations
they perceive and transcribe with perfect clarity.

—Meditation on *Holy Qur'an* 82:6–12

Morning Star

In the universal space below the seven heavens, behold, before
the first light of dawn, the brilliant morning star shines forth. To
grasp the spiritual secret revealed by this star, please notice its
piercing clarity, which penetrates every level of the mind and
senses. Thus it is that over each soul on earth there shines a perfectly pure angelic being, whose dear light penetrates all veils,
and who is appointed by Allah Most High as witness to every
thought and action.

—Meditation on *Holy Qur'an* 86:1–4

The Harmony of the Soul

Gaze upon this drama of manifest Being that radiates from
the Source of Being like overwhelming brightness from the sun.
Contemplate as well the subtle light of Revelation that re-
sembles cool and delicate streams of moonlight. The dynamic
brightness of Creation is displayed by Allah Most High during
the daytime of human knowledge, but remains veiled during
the luminous and peaceful night of Divine Mystery.

Behold the giant dome of stars and meditate on the Source of Power, Who shapes the cosmos with such intricate beauty. Envision the vast expanse of living earth, carefully prepared by the source of Life to bear fruit in abundance. And above all, contemplate the sublime harmony of the soul, enlightened by the Source of Love to discriminate clearly between mere sensual or intellectual intoxication and the path of true spiritual ecstasy. Those who remove the veils from their souls by practicing the holy way of life will find the incomparable treasure of Love. But those who allow their awareness to become drunk on limited, self-centered pleasure will fail to discover the limitless treasure.

—Meditation on *Holy Qur'an* 91:1–10

· COMMENTARY

Judgment: The Process of Cause and Effect

The Qur'an balances the ever-present experience of Creation's possibility with the experience of judgment: reaping the consequences of our actions here and now. In this sense, "time begins" at any moment that we live in attunement with our divine purpose, the process of becoming. "Time ends" whenever some event causes us to stop what we're doing and face up to the effects we have caused from a sense of self separate from the One. In this regard, the Qur'an frequently mentions the "day of judgment" (*maliki yaumadin*). This day can be any day, any moment, any small "death" that our limited self experiences, which can then lead us to reconsider and align ourselves with the Source of Being. "Most human beings perceive the end of time as far away, but the Ever-Present Source, above both time and eternity, knows the eternal Day to be near to every life with the most intimate nearness" (Sura 70:6–7).

In this sense, the Day of Truth and the Day of Creation are the same in the eternal moment of Allah. According to one story, the Prophet Muhammad, just before his passing, said to his followers, "I leave you two teachers—one speaking, the other silent. The speaking teacher is the·Qur'an. The silent one is the awareness of your own death." For this reason, the Sufis have for centuries attempted through contemplation to follow the advice of the Prophet's saying: "die before your death."

—Ed.

Divine Judgment

To Allah alone are clearly known the secrets of the inscrutable destiny of every being. Allah Most High knows from within every life lived on the land and beneath the sea. Not a leaf falls of which His embracing Awareness is unaware. There is not even a single grain of sand in the obscure depths of the earth, nor any plant, blooming or withering, that is not recorded in the Transcendent Qur'an, which is the perfectly clear Awareness of Allah.

My cherished human beings, this encompassing Divine Awareness receives you into sleep every night and knows intimately what you experience each day. Allah Most High thus sustains you moment by moment for a precisely destined time on earth and then calls you home into His Radiance, where the thoughts and actions of your entire lifetime are vividly revealed to you and are assessed in the Light of Truth.

The Resplendent Presence of Allah rules the hearts and protects the lives of His devoted servants. The All-Merciful One manifests angelic beings who watch carefully over human beings, recording every intention and every action. When the sleep of death overcomes the body, messengers from the Source of

Light appear in luminous forms to guide the soul through the terrifying maze of its own earthly thoughts and deeds. Eventually the soul emerges, pure and clear once more, into the Radiance of the Only Reality. By the mysterious command of Allah, each soul returns to its own True Source. This is the process of Divine Judgment, unerring and swift, which purifies and illumines all beings.

—Meditation on *Holy Qur'an* 6:59–62

The Marvelous Ship

The Power of Allah alone evolves the precious vessels which bear life upon this planet. The supreme vessel, the human body and mind, is like a marvelous ship. To sail sleek ships, running before the fresh wind, is exhilarating indeed. But when storms arise and huge waves break across these vessels, when human beings face suffering and death, only then do they remember to turn consciously toward Allah Most High. Only then do they realize the exalted way of Islam to be the complete offering of their individual lives to the Source of Life. Only then do they pray intensely with their whole being: "Most precious Allah, guide us safely through the storm and allow us to live the rest of our lives in constant gratitude."

When Allah Most Merciful responds to this prayer by guiding human beings again into calm waters, their spiritual intensity evaporates. Some even become arrogant and commit various wrongs against the precious life of humanity and against other creatures on the earth. My beloved Muhammad, please transmit this message to the careless and the complacent: "Listen, My heedless ones. Your indolent denial of the Ever-Present Source, this blind negation which leads you to assume the entire

universe to be yours alone, harms only yourselves. You may experience for a while your deluded enjoyment of personal power
that denies the Source of Power, but when you fall into the sleep
of death, you will be returned to the Living Truth, and the Ultimate Source, Who is now speaking, will reveal most vividly your
fundamental error."

—Meditation on *Holy Qur'an* 10:22–3

∽

Paradise and Hell

My beloved Muhammad, please encourage those who aspire to
Islam, which is the entire surrender of human life into Divine
Life, to recite daily with contentment of heart some of the verses
revealed to you in Arabic from the Eternal Book of Allah. No
one can dim or divert the power of the Divine Words that emanate from the Source of Power. Attempting to live apart from
the Source of Life, no being can find solace or refuge, for apart
from the Source of Life, nothing lives.

Please encourage those who aspire to Islam to be gentle
and selfless, to turn wholeheartedly toward the Source of Being,
and to call out to Allah Most Merciful every morning and evening,
longing only to gaze directly into the Face of Love. Tell these
aspiring ones never, for worldly ambition, to turn away from the
humble path that My lovers are demonstrating to humanity. Warn
them against listening to anyone who is infected by the negation
of Love, and whose heart and mind have thus been veiled from
the essential awareness of the Source of Love that allows one
truly to love. Because such persons follow only selfish impulses,
their lives are entirely out of harmony.

My beloved one, proclaim dearly to humanity: "Truth is

realized by turning toward the Ultimate Source alone, but human beings remain free to affirm or to negate."

Upon falling into the sleep of death, those who negate the Source of Love and whose lives have become infused with this negation will experience their return into the Splendor of Allah as entering a vast tent of fire, extending in every direction. Such living dreams of hellfire are more intense for those whose daily lives have expressed greater negativity. When these darkened souls call for the refreshment, which, during their earthly careers they have denied to others, they will be served dream water like molten copper that will scald their entire being. Thus, in the realm of limitless Radiance, the most terrible dreams of purification will occur to souls who here negate the Source of Light.

Plunging through the sleep of death, those who affirm the Source of Love and whose lives have been refined and exalted by this affirmation will not be tortured by restless and relentless dreams but will awaken immediately into Paradise, spiritually prepared by earthly careers turned toward the Source of Light to perceive the true nature of Allah's overwhelming Splendor. Already purified by every loving thought and action of their lifetimes, these souls will experience the resplendence of Divine Love as timelessly blossoming gardens of Eden flowing with rivers of peace. They will enjoy there the direct touch of Allah Most Merciful as mystic bracelets of gold and as mystic robes of delicate green silk embroidered with the golden thread of ecstasy. There they will enter sublime contemplation, resting on rich carpets of light and royal thrones of light.

Through whatever spiritual imagery it presents itself to purified vision, this boundless sphere of Paradise is simply the limitless Radiance of Divine Love. This is the most excellent of all the excellent gifts of Allah, the beautiful abode of illumination.

—Meditation on *Holy Qur'an* 18:27–31

The Careless Ones

The Ultimate Source, Who is now speaking, entrusts each soul with the highest responsibility it can bear. The outward actions and inward intentions of each soul, subtly recorded from before eternity in the Transcendent Qur'an, are evaluated with justice by Allah Most High. But many persons are not clear about this union of Divine Foreknowledge and human responsibility, and therefore engage carelessly in negative thoughts and deeds they believe will be ignored. Only when the Source of Power brings the Final Chastening upon these careless ones will they resort to prayer. But the belated prayers of such persons for Divine Mercy cannot be of any avail, for they will have made this Divine Cleansing necessary by heedlessly and even arrogantly turning away from My clear demonstrations of Love. By casually regarding My Holy Qur'an as one of the fables sung by poets, such persons have neglected to meditate deeply on the Words of Truth that not only flow through this Arabic Qur'an but are revealed to every generation and every nation. Those persons involved in the habitual negation of Divine Love cannot recognize you, My beloved, as an authentic Messenger from the Source of Love, and so they regard you as ambitious, mad, or possessed. You have brought them Living Truth, but they cannot bear Its penetrating Light.

If the Source of Truth left human beings alone to indulge ignorantly in their own selfish desires, the entire harmony of planetary life would be disturbed. Therefore, the Source of Wisdom continuously reveals the holy teaching that calls for constant remembrance of Truth. But many persons, lacking the necessary inward commitment, turn away from this path of continuous prayerful awareness.

My beloved servant and messenger, please inform your people that you do not look to any human being for support or acclaim, because the acclaim accorded you by your most precious Allah is infinitely more sweet, and Allah alone provides every support you need. Be assured that you are calling your people to nothing less than the Direct Path to the Ultimate Source of the Universe. Those who cannot trust that they will awaken from the sleep of death into the limitless Radiance of Allah are turning aside from this Direct Path. Even were the Source of Love to shower Mercy on those who turn away from Love, removing the suffering they have accumulated through their own negativity, they would continue to wander in blind negation of Love. They are fundamentally arrogant because they regard their own selfish desires as the central meaning of existence. Regardless of the suffering which Allah Most Merciful allows them to bring upon themselves during their earthly careers, these careless ones do not prayerfully submit their lives to the Source of Life, nor do their minds and hearts become even slightly humble. Therefore, the Supreme Source must bring upon them, during the sleep of death, that most terrible Divine Chastening which causes the Splendor of Allah to be experienced as endless fire. Walking through the final gateway of despair, they are at last humbled and eventually purified.

—Meditation on *Holy Qur'an* 23:62–77

The End of Time

Eternal souls are awakened from the momentary sleep of death by the pure Resonance of Allah, as clear and penetrating as a resounding trumpet. On that endless Day of Truth, souls no longer experience relationships of family or nation, nor do they feel any need to dispute about religious doctrines or practices. On this Day of Days those souls whose spiritual commitment has been truly substantial are heavy as gold when they are weighed on the balance of truth, and they live joyously in the Radiance of Allah. Those who have refused to awaken and to evolve spiritually during their earthly lives have no significant weight or substance, and they experience this very Divine Radiance as a fiery wind against the face of their entire being. All the negation in which they indulged during their earthly existence is now concentrated as a dreadful sullenness within their hearts.

The Voice of Truth chastens them: "Consider carefully. Were not My demonstrations of Love through the noble Prophets recited to you time and again, and did you not persist in dismissing them as mere imagination?" Still reluctant to assume responsibility for their own negation of Love, these souls respond evasively: "The intense suffering on earth prevented us from accepting any spiritual interpretation of life, and we were surrounded by people who were devoid of wisdom. Bring us now to Paradise, and if we continue to negate Your Love, this will really prove us to be ungrateful." Seeing through the self-deception and subtle arrogance of these souls, the Ever-Present Source powerfully responds: "Face your own negativity and cease to reason glibly with Me. Consider the devoted servants of Divine Love who surrendered to Me during their difficult earthly lives, praying constantly: 'Most precious Allah, we trust with our entire being the Words of Truth revealed through Your Messengers. Please bless us with Your sweet Forgiveness and heal us with Your merciful Touch, for Your Compassion is absolute.' You arrogant ones used My humble servants as objects for your laughter and derision, driving entirely from your own hearts and minds the life-giving remembrance of Allah Most High. Now,

on the august Day of Decision, while you undergo fiery purification, those surrendered souls who patiently endured your
negativity on earth are experiencing what you sense to be fire as
the glorious Radiance of Paradise. Their humility has become
their exaltation."

The Source of Wisdom questions the submitted souls who
awaken on the mystic Day at the end of time: "How many years
or eons do you think your body has lain beneath the earth in the
sleep of death?" The radiant souls reply with amazement: "Most
exalted Allah, we seem to have been sleeping but a single day, or
even less than a day." The All-Merciful responds: "Were your
awareness deeper, you would know that you entered the sleep of
death just an instant ago. Do you really imagine that Allah, Who
is complete Love, wishes loving souls to be separated from Him
for any period of time? Did you not realize that you would be
drawn back immediately into the Source of Love?"

—Meditation on *Holy Qur'an* 23:101–15

⁒

Day of Union

Do your people imagine that merely by claiming to believe,
without further suffering and testing, they will be counted among
the blessed ones who turn their whole being toward the Source
and Goal of Being? The Ever-Present Source leads even the most
deeply devoted souls through constant spiritual tests, helping
them to accurately assess whether they can live as well as contemplate the highest Truth. Through such trials, subtle traces of
hypocrisy are exposed and healed. Do those who secretly turn
away from Allah Most High imagine that they are confounding
the Source of Wisdom with their empty profession of belief?

How superficial is the understanding of those whose religion remains conventional!

My beloved one, as for those among your people who genuinely long to discover the Source of Love, you may assure them that their day of encounter and union is rapidly approaching, for Allah Most Wise is the embracing Awareness, Who already knows from within every desire of the heart.

Please make clear to your people that whoever struggles to live the holy way of life is doing so for spiritual development alone, not for the benefit of Allah Most High, Who is absolute Completeness and therefore does not need the submission or praise of any creature. Inform your people that those who turn with selfless devotion toward the Source of Love, for no reason other than Love, and who confirm this by transforming their entire lives into transparent expressions of Love, will be forgiven every negative thought and action. By the Blessing of Allah, these lovers will be brought entirely into accord with their own highest intentions and ideals.

The Source of Love has always taught human beings to express obedience and loving-kindness to their mothers and fathers. However, if parents attempt to divert children from commitment to the One Source by insisting on the worship or service of any limited forces or concepts, such parents can be loved but no longer obeyed.

On the Day of Union, when loving souls return into the Source of Love, they will experience perfect clarity regarding every detail of their earthly pilgrimage. On that infinite Day, those whose hearts and minds have affirmed the Ultimate Source and whose daily existence has expressed this affirmation in action will be led by Allah Most Sublime into the highest circle of spiritual companions, who are perfectly united with each other and merged entirely in Divine Love.

—Meditation on *Holy Qur'an* 29:2–9

Satan

My dear humanity, please listen carefully. The promise of Allah Most High that the noble way of Islam leads directly into Divine Radiance is the Living Truth. If your heart and mind remain grounded in this simple and essential certitude, the elaborate attractions of earthly life can no longer divert and defraud you. Continue to strengthen your spiritual commitment so that Satan, the deluding force of self-centered intelligence, cannot veil from you the Source of Wisdom. The subtle force called *Satan* is your only real enemy. Recognize clearly as dangerous adversary this living archetype of arrogance in all its manifestations. The call of Satan beguiles human beings into negating the Source of Love, and eventually leads them to that most terrible purification, the sleep of death, which dreams the magnificent Splendor of Allah to be an eternally blazing fire. This Final Chastening alone can clear away the chronic negation of Love. But those who live only by affirming Love, allowing this sublime affirmation to pervade all their thoughts and actions, will be soothed during earthly life by the healing forgiveness that flows from the Source of Love, and will awaken after the death of the limited self to the limitless treasure of Love.

My beloved Muhammad, your tender heart is concerned about those persons whose negative actions have been made to appear so beautiful by the force of delusion that they sincerely believe these actions to be good. Understand that Allah alone mysteriously leads those particular souls through spiritual distortion so they may draw upon themselves the experience of purification, just as Allah alone empowers other souls to resist the wiles of arrogance. My beloved, do not waste the strength of your being, which you should use to call humanity back to the

Source of Love, by lamenting the spiritual tendency of any person. Allah alone knows how to guide all souls, without exception, along the most mysterious path of purification, which returns them to their own True Source.

—Meditation on *Holy Qur'an* 35:5–8

⚭

The Unsurpassable Victory

Those who dedicate their lives to the loyal service of Love will be welcomed with unimaginable honor by Allah Most High into His boundless Divine Awareness, experienced by these souls as vast gardens of bliss where the fruits of wisdom flourish. These companions of Divine Love will gaze into each other's eyes as they recline with dignity and calm on royal thrones of profound contemplation. The holy cup of Love's communion will be passed continuously among them, filled from the cool and abundant fountain of Divine Presence. This delightful drink of sheer brightness opens the spirit entirely, without the slightest distortion of earthly intoxication. The Beauty of Allah Most High will be manifest as clear-eyed maidens, their ecstasy and purity of heart more rare and protected than eggs hidden away by great birds in deep desert sands.

Embracing in perfect spiritual friendship, these blessed souls converse together, resolving each other's most profound questions with Divine Wisdom. The Ever-Present Source, Who is now speaking, hears their words: "Cherished friend, what has become of that person who, during earthly existence, constantly mocked at my confidence in the guidance of the Holy Qur'an, ridiculing my conviction that when the body falls asleep in death, the soul awakens into eternal realms of subtle experience that mirror its temporal career?" The luminous companion replies: "Gaze for a moment into the lower realms of Divine Awareness." The soul looks and immediately recognizes that particular person, lost in the delirium that dreams of Divine Radiance as the fire of Hell. The spiritually exalted soul calls out to the soul being purified: "Greetings in the Holy Name of Allah Most Merciful. You are the one who attempted to undermine my conviction with your lack of conviction. Except for the blessings that flow from the Source of Love, I would be with you now in your terrible trial of purification. Now you know that there is a death beyond death, as well as a life beyond death. You must die entirely to the limited self. This is the meaning and purpose of your chastening. To lose oneself and to merge into Love is the unsurpassable victory. May all souls eventually attain this supreme union."

—Meditation on *Holy Qur'an* 37:40–61

&

The Day of Truth

Without the guidance of Divine Revelation humanity cannot truly sense the awesome reality of Allah Most Sublime. My beloved Muhammad, please teach your people to contemplate this way: On the Day of Truth, when the spectrum of manifest Being returns into the Clear Light of the Source of Being, the entire temporal realm of life-bearing planets will be lifted up in Allah's Hand of Power, and the seven heavenly planes of eternal praise will be gathered together in His Hand of Love. All the radiance of temporal and eternal Being streams from and returns to Allah alone, Who is infinitely more exalted than any human conception or description.

On the mystic Day, the Call of Truth will resound like a magnificent cosmic trumpet, and all creatures in the heavenly spheres and earthly regions will be thrown deep into ecstatic trance, save those who are in perfect conscious attunement with the Will of Allah Most High. Then the overwhelming Resonance of Truth will sound forth a second universal Call, and all the beings who have ever come into Being will awaken directly into the Presence of Allah and will rise up in the Resurrection of Love, gazing with awe upon the Source of Love. The spiritual earth upon which they stand will be composed purely of light from the Source of Light. The Transcendent Qur'an will descend like a brilliant sun. All the noble Prophets and the devout witnesses to their Prophethood will be gathered in radiant forms, and the variations among sacred traditions will be evaluated in the light of the Supreme Unity. No soul will be treated unjustly, and each will receive from Allah Most Merciful the eternal fruits of the particular level of wisdom and love it attained, for the Ultimate Source knows most intimately all that these countless souls have experienced.

—Meditation on *Holy Qur'an* 39:67–70

Argument

My noble Messenger, certain people will confront you, insisting: "There is nothing beyond or behind this present life. We live only in time and are swept away completely by time." But such persons have no firm, direct knowledge that human life is really what they suppose it to be. Their bold assertions are actually nothing more than empty conjectures. When they hear your recitation from the Book of Clarity, revealing the clear

demonstrations of Power and Love that have flowed from the
Ultimate Source throughout history, they will find no cogent
response. Desperately grasping for any argument to defend their
own narrow view of reality, they will challenge: "If your claims
are true, bring us our departed fathers to testify that there is life
after death." Do not engage in their superficial level of argument, but speak these Words of Truth, generously sharing with
those who argue vainly the deep knowledge you have received
directly from the Source of Wisdom: "My friends, the Source of
Life pours forth the rich experience of temporal life for the training of your eternal souls. When your particular spiritual education
is complete, the Source of Love calls you out of earthly life once
more. Allah Most High will gather all souls together at the end
of time to test their learning. There is not the slightest doubt
about this revealed Truth, but how few are those who really
understand."

—Meditation on *Holy Qur'an* 45:24–6

∾

Levels of Awareness

Do human beings imagine that those who respond wholeheartedly to the demonstrations of Love that proceed from the Source
of Love are on the same level of awareness as those whose negations of Love have become beautiful in their own eyes, and who
follow only their own circumscribed ideas and personal impulses?
As such persons live on very different levels of awareness during
earthly life, so will they exist in the realm beyond death.

Those immersed in authentic awe of Allah Most Sublime
live on the level of Paradise, the fragrant gardens of pure consciousness where four rivers eternally flow. Divine Clarity is the

river of transparent water, free from the slightest impurity, that refreshes the soul and slakes its thirst. Divine Knowledge is the river of sweet milk that nourishes the soul perfectly and never turns sour. Divine Bliss is the river of delicate wine that inebriates the soul who ascends in ecstasy. Divine Love is the river of clarified honey, the golden essence of mystical union. On the level of awareness called Paradise grow incomparable fruits, the countless Attributes of Allah Most High. There the soul is cleansed completely by the Divine Forgiveness that flows from the Source of Love. But on the level of awareness called Hell, the intense Splendor of Allah is falsely perceived as unbearable fire, and souls experience the terrors that they dream through their own chronic state of negation as boiling water which scalds their very being as they try to drink. My beloved, how can these two levels be compared?

—Meditation on *Holy Qur'an* 47:14–5

Final Testing

My dear human beings who are striving to attune your temporal existence to My Eternal Heart, do not allow family concerns or personal possessions to divert your inward attention from the constant remembrance of Allah Most High. Whoever inwardly looks away from the Ever-Present Source, even for an instant, loses precious spiritual strength and joy. Sustained and refreshed by ceaseless inward prayer and prostration to Allah Most Sublime, share generously and gratefully whatever has been provided for you by the Ultimate Source of the Universe. Or else you may suddenly encounter your moment of death, and cry out in lamentation: "Most exalted Allah, please allow my earthly existence to continue even a few days beyond its destined end, that I may at last offer freely from my possessions to those in need, and express at last to everyone the love within me, thus joining my life with the blessed ones whose lives are completely oriented toward the Source of Love." Allah Most High will not prolong, even for a moment, the earthly career of any soul whose time of final testing has come. Yet Allah Most Merciful is intimately aware of every compassionate action and intention throughout your entire lifetime.

—Meditation on *Holy Qur'an* 63:9–11

Stairways of Light

On the Day of Truth, those who have lived in negation of Love will face the awesome Divine Chastening, without any possible avenue of avoidance. The whole Creation wonders when the mystic Day will dawn, and this universal question is sent by countless minds and hearts up vast stairways of light toward the Source and Goal of Being. Angels and Archangels, making full use of their celestial power, can ascend these stairways to the Source during one heavenly day, which is equal to fifty thousand years of earthly time. My cherished human beings, do not imagine that you will come to know during your lifetime when the Final Day will arrive. Awaken instead to the deep inner patience that turns completely toward the Ever-Present Source and simply waits. The taste of this gift of perfect patience from Allah Most Merciful will be so sweet that you will not desire any spiritual experience beyond pure patience alone. Most human beings perceive the end of time as far away, but the Ever-Present Source, above both time and eternity, knows the eternal Day to be near to every life with the most intimate nearness.

—Meditation on *Holy Qur'an* 70:1–7

Destiny

My noble Messenger, when you are asked when the Day of Truth will arrive, please offer this profound spiritual teaching: "My friends, I do not know whether the endless and timeless Day promised by my most precious Allah will arrive within moments, or whether the Source of Power and Love will prolong the course of temporality for ages. As encompassing Awareness, Allah alone perceives the invisible and inconceivable destiny of every being, and the destiny of the entire Creation. This knowledge of destiny, which belongs to the Ever-Present Source alone, cannot be disclosed to any limited consciousness. Only chosen messengers whom Allah Most Merciful has turned entirely toward the Source of Love, and who are a delight to the Divine Heart, may receive various degrees of this panoramic Divine Awareness. Even then the Source of Wisdom sends angelic beings to watch over these messengers, helping them to convey with perfect accuracy their subtle messages from the Source of Truth. The Divine Presence alone inspires, guides, and accomplishes every thought and every movement of these totally surrendered servants of the Living Truth. Allah Most High has already taken careful account of every being and every event that will occur throughout time."

—Meditation on *Holy Qur'an* 72:25–8

The Moment of Illumination

When time suddenly disappears, in the eternal moment of illumination the brightness of the heavenly orbs will be extinguished by sheer Divine Splendor, and the universe will be split open and dissolved into transparent light. This full revelation of the Source of Light will blow away like mere motes of dust the primordial mountains, the cosmic structures upon which this earthly plane rests so securely.

This ultimate experience of transcending time comes inevitably to each soul, as the Voice of Truth now speaking has confirmed through all My noble Messengers. The promised Day cannot be delayed. What can human words and concepts teach in depth about this Day of Decision, this dawning of complete conscious submission, this merging of Being into the Source of Being?

My beloved Muhammad, clearly and compassionately remind humanity that those who fail to live in constant expectation of the mystic Day, regarding this teaching as myth or imagination, will be severely disappointed when the Last Day actually arrives and they are not spiritually prepared.

—Meditation on *Holy Qur'an* 77:8–15

The Call to Transformation

Upon the mysterious Day when time ends, all manifest Being will tremble at the first thundering blast of Divine Resonance that will utterly stop the world. The second wave of holy sound that washes over the entire universe will be the Call to Awakening.

At that timeless instant, every human heart that has ever pulsed with life will reawaken from its spiritual sleep, and all human eyes that have ever gazed into sunlight will be humbled, gazing instead into the overwhelming Splendor of Allah. Looking in surprise at their own luminous spiritual bodies, some awakening souls will exclaim: "Most exalted Allah, can it be true that we are actually being restored to human form, though our very bones have become ancient dust?" Shocked and confused by this spiritual resurrection, some disoriented souls will cry out: "Most exalted Allah, please do not return me to my limited human body!" But the Call to Transformation is irresistible, and this momentary terror will disappear when each soul realizes its spiritual body to be perfect, limitless, and holy. Then the soul will have truly awakened to the Radiance of Allah Most High.

—Meditation on *Holy Qur'an* 79:6–14

The Awakened State

When the Day of Enlightenment dawns, the soul, expressed as a luminous body, the face of its being suffused with calm joy, awakens into the supernal garden of Divine Presence, overwhelmed to comprehend at last the full significance of its own spiritual commitment. In this perfectly awakened state called Paradise, the sublime Resonance of Allah is experienced within the soul continuously, like a bubbling spring, without the slightest distracting sound of mundane thought or conversation. The soul finds waiting there the graceful chalice of unceasing prayer, the soft pillow and silken carpet of silent meditation, and the majestic throne of mystic union.

—Meditation on *Holy Qur'an* 88:1–15

⚮

Homecoming

These are the ineffably sweet Divine Words heard by the soul of Love at its homecoming into the Source of Love: "My beloved soul, having awakened at last into My Peace, you can now return consciously and completely to your own Original Source. As this homecoming fills you with inexpressible joy, it pervades Allah Most High with profound delight as well. Please enter now into eternal companionship with My most devoted servants of Love, and experience the perfect union with Love that is My highest Paradise."

—Meditation on *Holy Qur'an* 89:27–30

⚮

The Treasure of Love

The Source of Wisdom has mystically instructed humanity that the very Radiance of Allah Most High is experienced as the fire of Hell by souls who have become infected and pervaded by negativity. Those who consider the Words of Truth that descend perennially through My noble Prophets to be imagination or even prevarication must undergo this terrible purifying vision of Hell. Those who vehemently reject the existence of the Ultimate Source are turning their backs on the Source of Being, and thereby negating the very Ground of their own being. The souls who instead cherish awe toward Allah Most High and toward His Revelation will not fall into the delirium of hellfire upon entering the sleep of death. They are already purified by having lived the holy way of life with perfect trust and care, giving freely from their own wealth to those in need, and never granting favor or kindness to anyone from motives of personal gain or reward. These are the souls who seek only to turn toward the Source of Love and to delight the Divine Heart. They will certainly receive the entire treasure of His Love.

—Meditation on *Holy Qur'an* 92:14–21

Mother Earth

On the inconceivable Day of Truth, mother earth will be shaken by earthquakes, like the labor of a vast childbirth, and will bring forth those beings who have been sleeping and dreaming within her. Humanity will cry out: "What is happening to our great planetary mother?" On that Day beyond time, the totally transfigured earth of light will reveal all those who have fallen asleep within her in the sleep of death, empowered to do so by the Source of Power, Who is now speaking. On that timeless and transcendent Day, human beings will experience resurrection in bodies composed of light, and will be shown clearly all the thoughts and actions of their lifetimes. Those who have lived in harmony with the principles of justice and compassion, their very existence affirming the Source of Love, will receive the precise spiritual fruit of their actions and intentions, exact to the weight of a single ant. Those who have been drawn into various forms of the negation of Love will receive the experience of purification necessary to clear away that negation, measured with the precision that can weigh even an atom.

—Meditation on *Holy Qur'an* 99:1–8

✿

The Balance of Justice

On the Day of Truth, those souls whose earthly lives weigh heavy as gold on the balance of Divine Justice will receive their full inheritance of Divine Bliss. But those whose lives lack spiritual and moral substance will have no significant weight. These souls must plunge into the final and most radical purification, which causes the Splendor of Allah to be experienced as terrible fire. No words can convey the personal anguish through which the dross of arrogance and negation must be melted away.

—Meditation on *Holy Qur'an* 101:6–11

✿

True Spiritual Joy

My cherished humanity, constant rivalry over possessions and personal power can distract you entirely from the Ever-Present Source and from the holy way of life and prayer revealed by Allah Most High. But when the body is brought to the grave, all distraction ceases, and the soul must gaze directly into the consuming Light of Truth. Then every person will come to know with perfect clarity the eternal significance of human existence. Those who glimpse, while still on earth, the ultimate meaning of their thoughts and actions, will lead lives of intense caring and carefulness. Those who live totally selfish and careless lives that negate the Source of Life must eventually encounter Divine Radiance as the fire of Hell. Certainty here and now about this revealed Truth is by far the most valuable human possession. My dear humanity, at the dawning of the eternal Day souls will be

asked whether they have experienced only self-centered pleasure
or whether they know the nature of true spiritual joy. Consider
deeply what your response will be.

—Meditation on *Holy Qur'an* 102:1–8

The Afternoon of the World

This is the afternoon of the world, whose life has begun to
descend like the sun toward the final horizon where time ends.
Human beings are caught in this descending movement, except
for those whose minds and hearts constantly affirm the Source
of Love, and whose daily actions clearly express Love. These are
the intimate friends of Allah Most High, who encourage humanity to cherish the Living Truth and to remain patiently
committed to the holy way of ceaseless prayer and praise.

—Meditation on *Holy Qur'an* 103:1–3

Chapter Five

REVELATION

COMMENTARY

Religious Diversity

The Qur'an contains many comments about the diversity of human religions and the underlying unity of them all in one ground of reality. It says clearly that the message being given through the Prophet Muhammad is not a new one, and that Muslims should spurn any attempts to make it sectarian, cultic, or exclusive. "Please do not pay the least attention to any sectarian views, but courageously and openly proclaim to all: 'I affirm the truth of every Revelation which has come down as a Holy Book from the Source of Truth, and I am instructed by this very Source to be impartial among the peoples of Revelation. The Ever-Present Source, Who calls Itself by countless Divine Names, is the Source of our spiritual nation and your spiritual nations. We have our integral practice of the holy way of life, as you have yours. There need be no fundamental disagreement among us. Allah Most High will draw us all together as we return home to the Source of Love.'" (Sura 42:15).

Despite some Western views of Islam, and some more modern Islamic fundamentalist interpretations of it, the original message is simply and clearly one of harmony and tolerance.

—Ed.

91

⤝

The Prophethood of Muhammad

My beloved Muhammad, the Single Source has revealed Itself clearly through you, just as It did through My beloved Noah and all the other cherished guides of humanity. The Source of Wisdom now teaching humanity through you taught as well through My beloved Abraham, Ishmael, Isaac, Jacob, Jesus, Job, Jonah, Aaron, and Solomon. This very Source of Love sang the Psalms through My beloved David, and conversed directly with My beloved Moses. There are other Messengers of Allah whose holy lives have been revealed to you, My beloved, as well as many Prophets about whom you have not received precise revelation. These inspired and perfected human beings are all sent simply to bear joyous news of the homecoming into Paradise, or Divine Radiance, and to warn about the purifying fire of Hell, which is the very same Divine Radiance. So many of these luminous Messengers have emerged from the human family that there can be no impression that Allah Most Merciful has not spoken repeatedly to all nations. Allah is none other than boundless Power and complete Wisdom. And Allah Himself now bears witness that His Divine Words are pouring through you, My beloved Muhammad. The Ultimate Source has chosen you from before eternity to be the channel for the culmination of Revelation. The angels also bear witness to your noble Prophethood, yet no confirmation of this truth is necessary beyond that of Allah Most High, Who is Truth.

—Meditation on *Holy Qur'an* 4:163–6

&

Torah, Gospel, and Qur'an

The Supreme Source sent Jesus, son of My beloved Mary, to walk the noble way of all the Prophets, those deeply cherished guides of humanity. Through the Prophet Jesus, the Source of Wisdom transmitted the Radiant Gospel, full of the same Light of Truth that streams through the Living Torah, resonant with warning and guidance for those who turn with purity of heart toward Allah Most Sublime. The people of the Living Gospel, called Christians, can continue to live wisely in the light of the Revelation granted to them through My beloved Jesus. Only those are turning away from Allah Most High who abandon the wisdom that flows to their own people, through their own Prophets, from the Source of Wisdom.

The Eternal Source now reveals through you, My beloved Muhammad, this sublime Book of Truth, which confirms and safeguards the essential teaching of the Torah, the Gospel, and all the other authentic scriptures that existed before them. Thus Jewish and Christian traditions should be accepted reverently in the light of the Glorious Qur'an that descends gracefully through you. But you should not accept any teachings or practices of these earlier traditions which have sprung from limited human conceptions, or which contradict the clear principles of Truth revealed through the Holy Qur'an.

The Source of Life has shown the Prophets of all nations harmonious ways of life and open gateways into the Radiance of Allah. The Source of Power could have united all peoples into a single nation, but Allah Most Merciful has chosen to manifest His Truth through various sacred traditions as teaching and testing for human beings.

If each spiritual nation practices faithfully the path revealed through its own Holy Prophets, then all humanity will return together to the Source of Love. When time ends, on the Day of Truth, Allah alone will clarify the variations and contradictions among historical traditions. While abiding on the earthly plane of Being, evaluate the paths of Torah and Gospel in the light of this Living Qur'an that the Resonance of Allah is reciting through you. My beloved, never allow your people to be drawn away from the fundamental principle of Divine Unity by contrary teachings that other traditions may maintain. These are human distortions of previous Divine Revelations that remain essentially pure.

—Meditation on *Holy Qur'an* 5:49–52

Christians

My beloved, various people will bitterly reject the holy way of life revealed through you. You will discover that those called Christians are often most responsive to Islam as the Path of Love that returns directly to the Source of Love. Among Christians, you will find fully dedicated lovers of Divine Love who have renounced the world to live solely for Allah Most High. They will not be arrogant or exclusive when they hear the Words of Truth that have descended through the Prophet of Allah. You will see their eyes overflow with tears, as the deep recognition awakens that this Glorious Qur'an is the Living Truth. They will exclaim, "Most precious Allah, we experience spontaneous faith in Your Revelation through the Messenger Muhammad. Please inscribe our names among the blessed witnesses to the truth of Islam. Why should we Christians not also affirm the message of unity that the Source of Wisdom is transmitting through the Radiant Qur'an? Why should we not long to be embraced by Allah Most Merciful into the loving communion of Islam, the root and essence of all Divine Revelation?" Allah will respond with intense Love to the declaration of trust from His Christian lovers, and to their lives of sheer goodness, by bringing them home into the Source of Love, which they will experience as verdant gardens beyond time, flowing with rivers of purity and peace.

—Meditation on *Holy Qur'an* 5:85–8

The Infinite I Am

My beloved Muhammad, to the Supreme Source, Who speaks through you, belongs whatever is manifest as planetary or heavenly existence. Those whose entire lives intimately face the Source of Life never grow weary of being channels for Divine Power and are never too proud to serve as humble instruments of Divine Mercy, even in the smallest details of daily life. With every breath, these intimate friends of Allah Most High are ceaselessly praising the Source of Love, both during the common hours of the day and the secret hours of the night.

Many people mistakenly focus the transcendent worship natural to the human soul upon various etheric powers within Creation, using ritual objects shaped from substances of the earth, assuming that these crude talismans and the forces that they evoke can somehow awaken souls from the dark slumber of death into the radiant life of Paradise. Such indiscriminate worshippers should reflect carefully. Were there independent sources of spiritual power in the universe, rather than one Ultimate Source, they would be limited by each other and therefore would conflict, throwing into confusion all the realms of Being that now exist in perfect harmony. The worship which wells up spontaneously in the pure human heart should be offered consciously and directly to Allah Most High, the Single Source of boundless Power, Whose Throne is the unified field of Divine Energy and Who is beyond any possible description or conception. How foolish it is for beings whose understanding is partial to question the Source of Being, Who is total Wisdom. Allah alone is the One Who, through the penetrating Light of Truth, questions all persons concerning their actions and motivations, particularly those who turn away from the Ever-Present Source by imagining instead various separate sources of power.

My beloved, cry out to those who mistakenly worship the forces within relative existence: "Show me even one demonstration of Love that results from your reverence for these elemental and etheric forces. The way of true worship now being revealed through me is constant remembrance of the Ultimate Source alone. This is the same direct path of meditation without images and without limits revealed through all the Prophets before me. Yet many people still turn away, unwilling to face the Living Truth through continuous prayerful awareness, through constant submission of the limited self to its limitless Source."

Throughout the course of history the Source of Wisdom has sent Holy Messengers to bear only one essential message. Through these exalted and perfected human beings, the Source of Love calls into the heart of humanity: "There are no conscious beings separate from the infinite I Am that I am. Therefore surrender your very being to the Source and Goal of Being."

—Meditation on *Holy Qur'an* 21:19–25

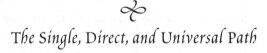

The Book of Reality

My beloved Muhammad, the Ever-Present Source, Who speaks through you, has revealed an uniquely authentic holy way to each and every nation, true spiritual disciplines that should be performed with care and constancy. Do not allow any other teaching to deflect your people from the dedicated practice of the noble way of life and prayer revealed through you. Please continue to invite all humanity to return together to the Source of Love. You can be absolutely certain that you are walking on the Direct Path of Allah's own Guidance.

If practitioners from other revealed traditions dispute with you, serenely reply: "Allah Most Merciful perceives with perfect clarity your intention to turn your life toward the Source of Love. On the mystic Day when you awaken from the sleep of finite existence, Allah Most Wise will explain clearly to you the diversity that now appears to divide His various Revelations. Do you not remember that the Ultimate Source knows most intimately the meaning of every event on the heavenly and earthly planes of Being? All has been recorded from before eternity in the boundless Book of Reality, the encompassing Awareness of Allah Most High."

—Meditation on *Holy Qur'an* 22:67–70

The Single, Direct, and Universal Path

My beloved Muhammad, the Voice of Truth has revealed to you precisely the same principles of Islam that were revealed to

My beloved Noah. The Ever-Present Source has transmitted to you the same inspired responsibility that was borne by My beloved Abraham, My beloved Moses, and My beloved Jesus. The Divine Message received by each and every Messenger is simple and clear: "Walk at every moment the exalted way of Islam, which is the constant merging of your individual life into the Source of Life, and do not allow conflicting views to develop concerning this single, direct, and universal path."

It can be extremely painful for those who worship cosmic or etheric forces to hear the transcendent Call of Islam that resounds through you. Do not be concerned if such persons vehemently turn away from your teaching, for Allah alone knows which souls will turn consciously toward their own True Source. Allah alone guides those who leave behind the negation of Love and take the mystic path of return into the Source of Love.

The nations who receive Divine Revelation through My Messengers often lose their human unity by indulging in conflicting views concerning this most precious knowledge of Divine Unity, becoming insolent and even violent towards one another. The Word of Power that radiates from the Source of Power has ordained human history as a precise temporal period for the testing and teaching of eternal souls. Were it not for this Divine Dispensation, Allah Most High would resolve immediately the foolish disputes within and among revealed traditions. Such superficially conflicting opinions about the same clear and universal Divine Message are poisonous to people who receive one of the sublime Revealed Books as an inheritance from the history of their nation, causing doubt and restlessness in their minds and hearts.

Therefore, My noble Messenger, you should call for profound harmony among all the Holy Revelations, and lead humanity as you have been led, along the single, direct, and universal path of Islam, which orients only toward the Ultimate Source. Please do not pay the least attention to any sectarian views, but courageously and openly proclaim to all: "I affirm the truth of every Revelation which has come down as a Holy Book from the Source of Truth, and I am instructed by this very Source to be impartial among the peoples of Revelation. The Ever-Present Source, Who calls Itself by countless Divine Names, is the Source of our spiritual nation and your spiritual nations. We have our integral practice of the holy way of life, as you have yours. There need be no fundamental disagreement among us. Allah Most High will draw us all together as we return home to the Source of Love."

After hearing these words of reconciliation which the Source of Wisdom empowers you to proclaim, if any persons continue to argue for divergent views concerning the Single Source, their arguments will be perceived by Allah Most High as specious and negative. By turning away from the Source of Love, these advocates of mere sectarian viewpoints are harboring hatred within their hearts which only the Divine Chastening can clear away. The Source of Truth alone sends down resplendent Books of Truth, and the Source of Wisdom alone provides the just balance upon which spiritual authenticity is weighed.

How few human beings understand the intensity and magnitude of the swiftly approaching Day of Clarification. Those who do not really comprehend the nature of the Last Day are impatient and would like to speed its arrival, whereas those who know the immense power of the Living Truth stand in trembling awe before the dawning of this infinite Day. Those who doubt or deny the onrushing end of time are simply living in the darkness of insouciance and error.

—Meditation on *Holy Qur'an* 42:13–8

⌘

The Religion of Truth

There are those even among the blessed People of Revelation, both Jews and Christians, who doubt the existence of the Ultimate Source, Who is now speaking. And practitioners from traditions which worship multiple divine beings become blind to the Single Source and Goal of Being. To demonstrate the Living Truth unequivocally to such persons, the Ever-Present Source sends as clear signs from Allah Most High completely purified human messengers, who selflessly transmit My Divine Words, which become the illuminating pages of Revealed Books, full of pure and just teaching.

But after these sublime pages of Revelation are received through My noble Prophets, their followers begin to disagree and become fragmented into religious factions. This is deeply regrettable because all nations are given precisely the same spiritual instruction from the Source of Wisdom: "Turn directly toward Allah alone and make your entire life a sincerely devoted offering to the Source of Life."

The Voice of Truth calls to human beings throughout history to turn around completely toward their own True Source, to plunge wholeheartedly into prayer each day, and to offer constant tenderness and assistance to those in any kind of need. This is the single Religion of Truth, natural to the human soul, which transcends all religious factions with its perfect clarity and directness.

—Meditation on *Holy Qur'an* 98:1–5

COMMENTARY:
The Prophets

Within the context of an underlying ground of Unity, the Qur'an re-introduces the reader to some of the prophets and messengers of the Middle East who preceded Muhammad. It mentions Jesus more often than any previous prophet and also contains portions of suras devoted to Adam, Noah, Abraham, Moses, Joseph, and others, some named and others unnamed. The selection of passages that Hixon renders here represents only a small portion of the whole. The prophets who gave a sacred book receive special attention, and so the Qur'an considers the "peoples of the Book" with equal honor. In a passage not rendered by Lex Hixon, the Qur'an says,

> Tell everyone: "We believe in the One Being, and what has been revealed to you, and what was revealed to Abraham, Ishmael, Isaac, and Jacob, and to the tribes, and what was given to Moses, Jesus, and all the prophets from their Source. We will make no distinction between any of them, and we resign ourselves to the same Source of All" (Sura 3:84, editor's translation).

The word for "prophet" in Arabic, *nabi*, need not indicate a person with a public mission. By one rendering, it can mean "one who gives forth what the divine spirit of Creation and abundance has given her/him." In this sense, the Qur'an calls each person to be Lover and Friend of Allah.

—Ed.

Teachings of the Prophet Noah

My beloved Noah turned toward the Ultimate Source and prayed: "Most precious Allah, following Your Guidance alone, I have reminded my people day and night to face the Ever-Present Source with their entire being, but the power of this persistent call has frightened them, and they take flight from the Living Truth. Whenever I invite them to accept the sweet forgiveness that flows from the Source of Love, they cover their ears, throw their robes over their heads as though seeking protection from burning sunlight, and heedlessly abandon themselves to habitual and mundane ways of thinking and acting.

"I address them openly in public places and also converse with them secretly in the privacy of their dwellings. Most exalted Allah, this is how I transmit teaching to my people from the Source of Wisdom: 'Dear friends, you need only turn consciously toward the Source of Love for the absolute Forgiveness of Allah Most High to pour into you and transform your entire existence. The Source of Life will then shower abundant blessings upon you, causing your lives to bear fruit in every way. You will have rains for your land, wealth and children for your family, and your experience of eternal joy and contentment will be like abiding in verdant gardens beside clear rivers. How can you fail to recognize and to trust implicitly the kindness of this wondrous Divine Power, Who brings you forth from your mother's womb and leads you through so many intricate stages of development?

"'Please try to appreciate how the Source of Power emanates the seven heavenly spheres of Being, each encompassed by another which is more subtle, placing in the universal space beneath these heavens the sun and moon as light for your physical eyes. As Allah Most High evolves the vehicle for your eternal soul from substances of the earth, so shall this physical body melt away again into the earth, that the spiritual body may spring forth once more from the Source of Light on a higher plane of manifestation. My people, this vast earth is a rich prayer carpet which Allah Most Merciful has carefully spread out for you. Every valley, broad or narrow, has been shaped by the Source of Power as a dwelling place or as a pathway for conscious beings.'"

—Meditation on *Holy Qur'an* 71:5–20

The Terrible Flood

The noble Prophet Noah proclaimed to his generation: "My people, it is no concern to me whether you find painful my persistent reminders of Allah Most High, because I live only for the Source of Life. I simply request that you deepen your resolve, clarify your minds, and decide whether or not you will follow me along the path of constant remembrance. If you decide to turn away, or even condemn me to death, I will not be disappointed, for I ask nothing from you, neither your wealth nor your gratitude. I seek support from Allah alone, having received the clear call to be among those whose lives are turned completely toward the Single Source."

The generation of My beloved Noah rejected him, regarding as mere imagination the Words of Revelation which poured through him. Therefore the Ever-Present Source, Who is now speaking, drew the Prophet Noah and his devoted followers into the ark of the secret heart to be vessels of Divine Love for all

Creation. But those who vehemently denied the demonstrations of Love streaming through Noah from the Source of Love were drowned in the terrible flood of their own negation. They were warned most compassionately by the Source of Being, but continuing to negate the very Ground of their own being, they could no longer really be.

—Meditation on *Holy Qur'an* 10:71–3

✢

The Path of the Prophet Abraham

Allah Most High does not dispel instantly the severe distortion of mind and heart caused by worshipping mental or cosmic forces, the false worship that turns away from the One True Source. Other moral distortions are healed simply by the sweet forgiveness that overflows eternally from the Source of Love. But whoever attempts to elevate limited concepts and experiences to the level of Divine Truth has strayed deep into the shadows of error.

My beloved Muhammad, your own people prayed to etheric forces not even at the level of lower heavenly beings, elemental energies themselves not even aware of the Supreme Source, Who is now speaking. Other peoples pray to various personifications of the cosmic rebel Satan, the higher intelligence that is powerful and compelling, but that turns away from the Ultimate Source by claiming ultimacy for itself.

Before time began, this Satanic arrogance declared to Allah Most High: "With my brilliant power and eloquence, I will draw to me a portion of Your precious human servants by convincing them that their own intelligence is ultimate and needs look to nothing beyond itself. I will fill them with brilliant notions of how to take the forces of the universe into their own

hands. Invading them and dwelling within them as these intoxi-
cating ambitions, when I command, human beings will attempt
to change the very laws and principles of Your Creation."

Whoever trusts as a companion this disintegrating force
called Satan, instead of making friends with the Source of Love,
has suffered devastating loss. This should be obvious to everyone. Those who become intoxicated by Satan's beguiling promise
that human intelligence and ambition are ultimate will experience the very Radiance of Allah as the relentless fire of Hell. But
those who keep free from this dangerous intoxication by turning
constantly toward their own True Source, living day by day the
harmonious life of Islam, will be drawn by the Source of Love
directly into Divine Love, which they will experience as timeless
gardens flowing with rivers of ecstasy and tranquility. This homecoming into the Source of Love is Allah's Promise. Who could
be more truthful than the One, Who is Truth? This message is
not your imagination, My beloved Messenger, nor was it the
imagination of countless Prophets before you who brought My
Words of Truth to their people. Whoever turns away from the
Source of Love and spreads the negation of Love will inevitably
experience painful results, and will eventually be utterly alone,
without a single friend. Only Allah Most Merciful will be able to
help, if such a person is still able to face Allah. But the man or
woman who lives life completely turned toward the Source of
Love, affirming Love with every breath, will encounter Paradise
everywhere and will begin to understand the justice rendered to
all beings by Allah Most High, justice so perfect that no soul is
wronged by even so much as the point of a date stone.

Who could walk a more beautiful spiritual path than the
person who lovingly surrenders all to the Source of Love, becoming one whose daily life in every detail clearly expresses Divine
Love? This is the original path of the Prophet Abraham, who

turned with purity of heart to the Source of Purity and whom
Allah Most Sublime embraced as His most intimate friend.

—Meditation on *Holy Qur'an* 4:116–25

The Enlightenment of the Prophet Abraham

My servant and messenger Abraham confronted his kinsmen:
"You are elevating elemental forces to the rank of angelic beings,
invoking these forces through ritual objects, and worshipping
them to obtain power. I can clearly see that your lives and the
life of our people are being severely distorted by such practices."
The Source of Wisdom, Who is now speaking, placed from before eternity this penetrating spiritual understanding in the soul
of My beloved Abraham so that he would be a leader for all
those who turn with perfect clarity toward Allah alone.

The highest Truth, that the Ever-Present Source alone truly
exists, was shown to the Prophet Abraham in this way. While he
was immersed in solitary contemplation, within the vastness of
the evening sky the first star suddenly appeared. To the pure
vision of the Prophet, the star's light revealed the entire universe
as the luminous manifestation of Allah's Majesty. While My intimate friend Abraham meditated on the bright mirror of my
Creation, the evening star moved across the sky and disappeared
behind the mountain. Perceiving this as clear teaching from the
Source of Wisdom, he reflected: "Allah's Majesty cannot be loved
as totally as one loves His Essence."

Then the full moon rose. Ascending further in contemplation, Abraham exclaimed: "Behold a mystic symbol for the
transcendental beauty of Allah." But his meditation on Divine
Beauty also came to an end as the moon disappeared behind the

mountain. Recognizing once more a teaching from the Source of Wisdom, he prayed intensely: "Most precious Allah, please guide me beyond Your Majesty and beyond Your Beauty, or I will remain among those who do not awaken to the highest Truth."

Having supplicated the Supreme Source for guidance the whole night through, my intimate friend witnessed the magnificent desert sunrise. Perceiving the sun's vast radiance as a teaching from the Source of Wisdom, he declared: "Behold a mystic symbol for the Power of Allah." All day long he remained plunged in contemplation of Allah Most High as transcendent Power, but when the fiery sun finally set, his adoration of the Divine Attributes disappeared, and he awakened mystically into the Divine Essence alone.

After returning from the wilderness to his people, the Prophet Abraham proclaimed: "I have always been free from religious practices that exalt forces of nature. But now I have been brought face to face with the Essence of Allah, the Only Reality, Who alone radiates the broad expanse of earth and heaven. I have lost myself and found my Prophethood in the truth that Allah alone exists."

The people disputed bitterly with their Prophet, threatening him with the wrath of the various etheric forces which they worshipped. Displaying the utter calm of illumination, Abraham replied: "Do you imagine that any threat or argument could turn me away from the Ultimate Source when I am experiencing direct guidance from the Source Itself? I fear no powers in the universe, for I have always turned toward the Source of Power. Have you forgotten that the encompassing Awareness of Allah manifests and harmonizes the entire Creation? How could I fear the hatred of any being when I am receiving constant inner assurance from the Source of Love? You are the ones who should be apprehensive, my people, having elevated your own limited concepts and experiences to the level of divinity. They can offer you no ultimate support or refuge. Consider carefully which of us is receiving true protection. Only those who turn solely toward the Source of Love and do not obscure their being by the slightest negation of Love are perfectly guided."

My beloved Muhammad, such was the illumined insight that the Source of Wisdom transmitted through the Prophet Abraham for the instruction of all humanity. The Ever-Present Source alone draws hearts and minds to higher and higher levels of vision and understanding. Allah Most High is encompassing Awareness and complete Wisdom.

—Meditation on *Holy Qur'an* 6:74–83

The Prophet Abraham Teaches His Kinsmen

My beloved Muhammad, please recount to your people the teaching of the noble Abraham, a truly complete human being, a Holy Prophet, and the intimate friend of the Supreme Source, Who is now speaking. Courageously, the Prophet Abraham confronted his kinsmen: "Why do you worship mere artifacts, crude representations of divinity which cannot hear your innermost prayers or guide your spiritual development, and from which no transforming power flows? My dear kinsmen, sublime knowledge such as you cannot imagine has been poured from the Source of Wisdom into my mind and heart. Follow with me this Living Guidance and we will be led together on the exalted way of Islam that directly faces the Source of the Universe. Please do not cling to your own limited concepts and experiences, for that is the path of the cosmic rebel Satan, who exalts his own intelligence above the Revelation sent from the Source of Truth. My kinsmen, if you continue to turn away from the Source of Creation by worshipping limited expressions of power within Creation, I fear you must share the arrogant delusion of Satan and enter the terrible sphere of Divine Chastening."

The elder kinsmen of My beloved Abraham replied: "What blasphemy are you suggesting? To turn away from the primeval deities of desert and mountain? If you do not submit to their authority, you shall have to be stoned. Remove your family from our clan immediately, or we will be forced to enact the ancient judgment of death against our own children." Abraham responded from the inward depth of his noble Prophethood: "May the peace that flows from the Single Source of the Universe be with you, my kinsmen. I pray that the Source of Love will heal your hearts with the sweetness of His Forgiveness, for Allah Most High graciously fulfills the wishes of those who are turned completely toward Him. I will now lead my family and loyal followers far away from your ancestral household and from the elemental forces which you worship. We will live in reliance upon the Ultimate Source alone. Turning wholeheartedly toward Allah, may my people always be accorded abundance and protection."

Because My Messenger Abraham expressed the strength of his conviction by abandoning his ancestral clan and their limited religious practices, the Ever-Present Source presented to him as exalted child and grandchild My beloved Isaac and My beloved Jacob, both of whom were awakened into Prophethood by Allah Most High. The Source of Love placed the complete treasure of Love within these great souls, who will be remembered and honored always by those who love the Living Truth.

—Meditation on *Holy Qur'an* 19:41–50

⨍

The Sacred Lineage of the Prophet Abraham

My noble Messenger, please teach humanity to contemplate the courageous action of the Prophet Abraham, and of those whose hearts were joined with his, when he proclaimed to his people: "We are liberated from the spiritual bondage of your way of life, which relies upon the superstitious propitiation of elemental forces, and thus ignores the Ultimate Source of the Universe. We cannot have confidence in you as a people grounded in the Living Truth, and there can never be reconciliation between us until you turn your hearts and minds toward the Single Source." Yet My beloved Abraham felt compassion for his kinsmen, and assured them: "Friends and elders, I will pray constantly to the Source of Light for your spiritual illumination, but I can never condone your foolish turning away from the Ever-Present Source."

Please instruct all those who inherit the sacred lineage of the Prophet Abraham to pray this way: "Most precious Allah, may we turn toward Your Divine Mystery in ever deeper trust and humility until we complete the immense journey, the conscious return into Your original Radiance. Most exalted Allah, divert from us please the negativity of those beings who turn away from the Source of Being, and liberate us from our own negativity with Your absolutely forgiving love. You alone, Allah Most Sublime, are boundless Power and complete Wisdom."

The family and followers of the noble Prophet Abraham serve as profound inspiration to all who await the Day of Illumination, the mystic return into the Radiance of Allah Most High. Whether or not human beings turn away, Allah alone remains the Source and Goal of Creation, needing absolutely nothing yet graciously receiving the endless praise that flows spontaneously from all hearts. At any moment, it is possible that the Source of Love, Who is now speaking, will reconcile through Divine Love those who are existing in the mode of negation, for Allah Most High is awesome Power blended with sweet Forgiveness and most tender Mercy.

—Meditation on *Holy Qur'an* 60:4–7

&

The Mystical Dream of the Prophet Joseph

Manifesting through the spiritual transformation of the Arabic alphabet, the verses of this Luminous Qur'an clarify the entire universe. The Ever-Present Source thus reveals eternal meaning through the medium of time as the resonant chanting of the Arabic Qur'an, so that humanity can awaken and truly understand.

My beloved Muhammad, the Source of Wisdom will now communicate through you the most beautiful history of Divine Guidance in this Living Qur'an, the saga of the noble Joseph. Without awakening to the mystical significance of this drama, one cannot know the sublime spiritual stature of the human soul.

As a child born to the mystic way, My beloved Joseph was blessed with dreams and visions. He confided them to his father, whose prophetic wisdom was profound. Sharing his most significant spiritual experience, the radiant child Joseph whispered: "My dear father, I saw eleven stars with the sun and moon together in the sky. They bowed deeply before me." The intuitive and divinely inspired father perceived here the promise of many Holy Gifts, the very least of them being the vast earthly power his son would someday wield in the Kingdom of Egypt. He cautioned: "My precious child, do not relate this vision to your brothers or to any other person. It is too awesome to accept. They may attempt to discredit or even to kill you. My son, the proud intelligence who originally refused the Divine Request to bow before Adam became the cosmic rebel Satan, and has since infected the human mind with blind arrogance. Allah Most High has chosen you and healed you from that blindness. Allah Most Wise will teach you inwardly the interpretation of dreams, even the interpretation of the very dream of Creation. Allah Most Merciful will exalt you to the height of perfect blessedness, where you will merge into the Source of Love, opening the mystical door of the House of Jacob so that the Power of Revelation may flow into your generation. My dearest child, this blessedness and holy mission were entrusted to your revered spiritual ancestors, the noble Abraham and Isaac. This mission is the progressive awakening of humanity to its essential perfection initiated through the transcendental Adam, before whom even the angels bowed with their whole being, as stars, sun, and moon bowed before you in your vision. Yes, dear Joseph, the secret essence of the human soul is the encompassing Awareness and complete Wisdom of Allah."

—Meditation on *Holy Qur'an* 12:1–6

The Call of the Prophet Moses

Beloved Muhammad, please transmit the history of how My Prophet Moses was called directly to the Source of Light, Who is now speaking. Observing a brilliant glow upon the mountainside, the noble Moses told his family: "Remain here beside our tents. I will explore the mountain for the source of this splendor. Perhaps there will be only smoldering brands from a brush fire, or perhaps I will encounter powerful Divine Guidance."

When the Prophet Moses discovered and approached the awesome flames, the Voice of Allah resounded clearly through them: "My beloved Moses, I am Allah Most Sublime. Approach Me barefoot and do not cover your heart or mind with the slightest mundane veil, for you stand now in the mystic valley of revelation. The Ever-Present Source, the all-embracing I Am, has called you here. Open your entire being to these resonant Words of Truth. The highest Truth is that I alone am. Therefore, offer your life-breath only to Me, and perform from this day forth that continuous prayer which is the inward remembrance of Me. The experience of directly facing the highest Truth will come inevitably to every soul, but Allah Most Merciful conceals this destiny so that each soul will make its own sincere efforts to reach the Living Truth and receive the precious fruits of those efforts. My noble Messenger, let not those who doubt and who are insouciant distract your people from the swiftly approaching Moment of Truth. Those who live as though the Creation were somehow their own personal caprice are losing their lives by turning away heedlessly from the Source of Life."

Thereupon the Source of Power asked His Messenger: "What are you holding in your right hand?" Moses humbly replied, "Most precious Allah, this is my staff. When tired, I lean upon it. I strike the branches of the trees with it, scattering green leaves to feed my sheep. I use it in many practical ways." Allah Most High called into the heart of His Prophet: "Cast your staff upon the earth." As he obeyed, the wooden staff became sheer spiritual energy, moving like a luminous serpent. Again Allah spoke within the secret heart of His devoted servant: "Take hold of this Holy Energy fearlessly, and then your staff will appear again in its mundane form. Carry it as a living conduit of My Power. But first place your right hand against your breast until bright light streams forth from your palm. Then bear the staff of power with the hand of purity. These are clear signs of My Divine Presence, but the Supreme Source will open your eyes to much greater demonstrations of Love and Power. My beloved Moses, you are to confront and to subdue the Pharaoh of Egypt, the archetype of human arrogance."

The Prophet Moses prayed from the very depths of his being: "Most precious Allah, open my mind and heart fully in preparation for this task. Unravel the knots of my speech, that Your Words of Truth may flow through me unimpeded and awaken clear understanding. Anoint with Your Power one from my family, my dearest brother Aaron, to lend his strength to mine and to be with me intimately throughout my mission. Together we will sing Your praises with joy and keep your resplendent Presence constantly in our awareness. Most precious Allah, only You know how inseparable I am from Aaron, as both of us are inseparable from You."

The Resonance of Allah responded: "Your prayers are fully and instantaneously granted. The Source of Wisdom has most carefully guided and guarded you, from the moment when Allah Most Merciful spoke these Divine Words within the heart of your mother: 'Place your baby in an ark, and fearlessly set him afloat on the flowing river. He will be found and taken to one who is blind to the Ultimate Source, but the child will be protected.' Since then, My beloved Moses, the Source of Love has directed loving care toward you constantly, clothing you in the raiment of Love that you might develop inwardly and walk securely along your destined path to this powerful moment of Divine Calling."

—Meditation on *Holy Qur'an* 20:9–39

The Prophet Moses Confronts Pharaoh

The Voice of Truth called these words into the secret heart of My beloved Moses: "Journey to the region of those who deny their own True Source. There you will confront Pharaoh, who is the archetype of human arrogance. Discover if anyone in the realm of Egypt is still able to turn with awe and purity of heart toward the Ultimate Source of the Universe." The noble Moses responded humbly: "Most precious Allah, those in power will consider me mad or possessed. My heart may be frozen with fear and my tongue may not be released to speak Your Holy Words. I have committed a crime in Egypt, and they may put me to death. My brother Aaron is better suited for this mission." Allah Most High further illuminated the heart of His Prophet: "My beloved Moses, yours alone is the call. My Demonstrations of Power will be with you. The Source of Power will hear your every prayer, guiding and protecting you in ways more subtle than you can understand. Proclaim to Pharaoh: 'I come bearing truth as a humble messenger from the Source of Truth, the Creator and Sustainer of the Worlds, Who wishes freedom for His cherished ones, the Children of Israel.'"

The Prophet Moses made the arduous journey and courageously delivered the Divine Proclamation. Pharaoh responded: "Moses, did we not lavish our favor upon you since childhood? Yet you committed an act of murder and now show us no gratitude." My Prophet replied: "I committed that crime before my whole life was turned consciously toward the Living Truth. I fled from you, fearing your wrath. But the Source of Truth has enlightened me since then with profound understanding, awakening me as His servant and messenger. Pharaoh, is this the favor you have conferred on me, to enslave my entire people?"

Perceiving the new strength and radiance of this foster child, the Pharaoh asked: "What is this Source of Truth you speak about?" The noble Moses replied: "There is but One Ultimate Source behind whatever you discern in the heavens or on the earth. This truth of unity can be immediately experienced by affirming the Ever-Present Source with your entire being. Pharaoh, this is your own True Source, as well as the Source of your ancient ancestral line."

The avowed adversary of Allah turned to his advisors and declared in derisive tones: "This messenger who claims to have been sent to us has clearly been possessed by some wandering spirit." Whereupon My Prophet Moses once more courageously affirmed: "There is only One Original Power, Who rules in the East, the West, and every other region. This truth can be experienced by attributing Reality and Majesty to the Ultimate Source alone." Then the Pharaoh, who had transformed himself into an instrument of negation, began to respond aggressively: "If you accept any authority above me, I will have you imprisoned for blasphemy." Moses interjected calmly: "Would you act so hastily if I could show you a convincing demonstration of Power from the Source of the Universe?" Seething with anger, Pharaoh replied: "Demonstrate to us that you speak accurately."

So My beloved Moses cast down his staff, as he had been instructed by the Source of Power, and it was transformed into a flow of spiritual energy like a luminous serpent. He placed his right hand against his heart, as instructed by Allah Most High, and bright light streamed from his upheld palm before the eyes of the whole assembly. Pharaoh called together his advisors: "Moses has become a sorcerer. With this magical power, he will attempt to destroy our authority and appropriate our wealth. What action should we take against him?" The advisors replied:

"O supreme Pharaoh, cause to be gathered from the entire Land of Egypt the most adept sorcerers, and arrange between them and Moses a battle of power which he will certainly lose." So sorcerers and shamans were assembled, along with the populace, on an auspicious day. The people promised their religious allegiance, and Pharaoh promised his special protection and favor, to the adepts in magic who would be victorious.

The noble Moses invited his opponents to generate their power first. With complex spells and arcane rituals, they threw their magic sticks and magic ropes, crying out: "Through the sacred authority of the supreme Pharaoh we will be victorious." Then my servant Moses, with the dignity and calm of perfect submission, cast down his simple shepherd's staff, which was transformed into a wave of spiritual energy that surrounded the elaborate implements of the shamans in brilliant light and neutralized their hypnotic powers. The genuine adepts were so profoundly impressed that they bowed low and exclaimed: "We turn in obedience to the Source of Power Moses and Aaron worship."

Pharaoh bellowed with rage: "You have offered your allegiance before I, the supreme Pharaoh, have given permission. You have conspired with Moses to practice this deceptive sorcery. But now you will witness real power. I will have your hands and feet cut off, and the rest of your body crucified." The adepts replied with the intense conviction awakened in them by Allah Most High: "You cannot harm our souls with such torture, Pharaoh, for we have turned our entire being toward the Source of Being, unto Whom all must return. We pray to the Supreme Source to forgive our countless acts of turning away. May we be the first among our nation consciously to face the Living Truth."

The Ever-Present Source then revealed these Words of Guidance in the heart of the Prophet Moses: "Escape with My devoted servants in the darkness of night. You will be pursued by the warriors of the wrathful Pharaoh." The royal guard indeed spread out across the land in search of My Prophet and his loyal companions.

Gardens of Divine Abundance, fountains of Divine Love, treasures of Divine Wisdom, and the nobility of Divine Life—both in Paradise and reflected upon the earthly plane of existence—are subtly removed by Allah Most High from all arrogant persons, who are called People of Pharaoh, and are conferred instead upon persons who have consciously surrendered to the Ultimate Source and who are called Children of Israel.

Beside the Red Sea at sunrise, the companions of Moses sighted Pharaoh's army and cried out: "We will be overtaken!" Whereupon the Voice of Truth spoke within the pure heart of His Messenger: "Strike the raging sea of this world with the staff of Prophecy." The miraculous power released by this inspired action opens safe passage through the dangerous ocean of earthly life into the Source of Life, delivering forever those who sincerely follow the Light of Revelation, while the army of arrogance and negation is drowned.

Such incontrovertible demonstrations of Power and Love flow constantly from the One Source. Yet how few persons experience the truth of this clear demonstration in their own lives.
—Meditation on *Holy Qur'an* 26:10–69

The Enlightenment of the Prophet Moses

Having entrusted the spiritual leadership of the people to his brother Aaron, exhorting him to live in purity of heart free from the slightest negation, the noble Prophet Moses responded to My Divine Call and ascended the mountain.

When My beloved Moses had completed the destined forty nights of his solitary retreat, the ultimate moment arrived on the final night, when he could converse directly with the Supreme Source, Who is now speaking. With great intensity, he prayed: "Most precious Allah, please remove every veil from my eyes that I may perceive You as You truly are." Allah Most High responded by placing these Divine Words in the heart of His Prophet: "You will not be able to maintain your personal awareness when you encounter My Radiance, for not even this mountain could withstand the direct encounter with Divine Light." Then the Source of Light revealed Its full Resplendence to the inner vision of the noble Moses, who felt that the very mountain on which he stood had disintegrated into dust, as his personal awareness was lost in Divine Splendor.

When My beloved Moses regained consciousness of the world, he had awakened fully to his Prophethood, and immediately prayed: "Most precious Allah, the praise arising spontaneously from the minds and hearts of all beings is directed only to You. Turning wholeheartedly toward You, I am the first of my generation to experience You directly as the Only Reality." Allah Most Merciful responded within the heart of His noble Messenger: "Yes, I have selected you from among all human vessels to pour into you My sublime Message for humanity and the transforming Power of My Very Words. Now receive with gratitude through your personal awareness what streamed into your soul while you were lost in ecstasy."

The Source of Wisdom manifested then to the purified vision of the Prophet Moses radiant tablets containing the subtle principles of the holy way of life and the spiritual meanings of all beings and events. Allah Most Wise called within the heart of His Prophet: "My noble Messenger, return now to your people, bearing this vast body of sacred knowledge. With strength and courage urge them to express these fundamental principles in their daily existence. I will show you clearly that those who refuse to transform their lives into channels of My Holiness must remain imprisoned within their own suffering. This profound demonstration of Divine Love which you bring, I will conceal from those who walk the earth with arrogance, committing injustices against humanity and against the life of the planet. Even though these arrogant ones may hear the Words of Truth which descend through you, they will remain unable to understand unless they become humble. Even though they may see people joyously living the holy way of life, they will not be able to recognize it as a fruitful path unless they become humble. These arrogant ones will perceive instead the way of selfishness as the best path, because they ignore and even consciously negate the demonstrations of Love that are flowing constantly from the Source of Love."

—Meditation on *Holy Qur'an* 7:142–6

Moses Meets a Wandering Sage

My beloved Muhammad, please convey this secret history as spiritual instruction for all humanity. While traveling through the wilderness, the noble Moses once encountered a perfectly surrendered servant of the Ultimate Source. The Source of Love had entirely flooded the heart of this mysterious servant with Divine Compassion. This rare soul had received the mystical knowledge that flows directly from the Ever-Present Source. Recognizing this solitary desert wanderer to be thoroughly enlightened, My beloved Moses sought permission to follow him: "Revered sage, I wish to study with you the profound wisdom that you have been taught so intimately by the Source of Wisdom." The sage replied: "There is no way for you to bear my companionship without protest, because my way of life transcends the present development of your spiritual understanding." Moses responded: "Revered sage, if Allah Most High ordains this experience as instruction for humanity, I will try to bear your teaching patiently and without protest." The illumined one replied: "Then follow me for a while, as Allah has ordained, but under no circumstances question my actions until I myself interpret them for you." So this remarkable teacher and his remarkable student wandered away together into the wilderness.

Reaching the seacoast, they boarded a ship almost ready to sail. The noble Moses, responding in the way Allah ordained, was shocked to see his mysterious companion breaking a small hole in the boat's hull and cried: "The innocent passengers on this ship will be drowned. You appear to have committed an outrageous act!" The enlightened sage calmly replied: "Did I not warn that you would be unable to endure my teaching?" Moses responded with dignity: "Revered master, please forgive me and keep me in your hallowed company."

After leaving the seacoast, they encountered a young man on the road. With terrible suddenness, the sage took the life of this youth. Responding as Allah Most High ordained, My servant Moses again cried aloud: "Without any justification, you have murdered an innocent person. You appear to have committed a despicable act!" Once again the intimate friend of the Living Truth simply replied: "Did I not warn that you would be unable to endure my teaching?" Moses, who could clearly perceive the inward perfection of this enigmatic person, replied with humility: "Revered one, you have been extremely patient with me. If I question you even once again, please send me on my way."

So the profound teacher and his profound student walked the dusty road until they reached a walled stronghold, where they asked for food and drink but were refused hospitality. Part of the encircling wall was about to tumble down, and the two labored long and hard to rebuild it. Responding as Allah Most High ordained, Moses asked: "Master, why engage in such intense labor without any compensation?" The friend of Truth then firmly proclaimed: "You must leave me now, my brother. As I warned, you cannot bear patiently with my way of life, which moves in total submission to the most mysterious Mercy of Allah. Before you depart, please accept as a gift from the Source of Wisdom the proper interpretation of my actions.

"The ship provides livelihood to certain seafarers who are devoted to Allah Most Merciful. A pirate vessel, passing there today, is seizing every crew along its path and putting them to the sword. But the breach in the hull will be discovered and that ship will not set sail.

"The young man, child of devout lovers of Allah Most Merciful, was turned away completely from the Source of Love, treating his parents with insolence and even dangerous cruelty. My most precious Allah desires to protect this soul from complete self-destruction and to grant his parents instead a child who will develop profound compassion and purity of heart.

"Within the crumbling wall there is hidden a treasure not yet to be exposed which belongs to two orphans whose father lived most devotedly the holy way of life. My most precious Allah desires that these children, only when they have come to full strength and maturity, should discover the wealth that their father has left for them.

"Every action is the spontaneous expression of the most subtle Mercy that flows from the Ever-Present Source. I act with absolutely no illusion of personal motivation. This, my dear

brother Moses, is the mystical knowledge by which my entire
being has been illuminated."

—Meditation on *Holy Qur'an* 18:65–82

⚮

The Life of Jesus as Revealed to Mary

The angels called: "Dearest Mary, listen. Allah Most High sends
you joyous news of the Divine Word, emanating directly from
the Source of Love, whose mystical name is Messiah and who
will be known as the noble Jesus. He will be profoundly honored in this world, and in the realm of Paradise he is eternally
beloved, abiding with the most intimate companions of Love,
deep within the Radiance of Allah. The Messiah Jesus will transmit Truth to humanity, beginning as an infant in his cradle and
continuing until he reaches manhood. He will be utterly righ-
teous and pure of heart."

The Virgin Mary turned directly to the Ultimate Source
and prayed: "Most precious Allah, how can I bear a child, since
no man has known me?" Allah Most Merciful then awakened
Mary spiritually by placing these Divine Words in her heart:
"My beloved Mary, the Source of Power can manifest whatever
is needed to guide humanity. To project any being or event, Allah simply affirms it and it is. Through your spontaneously
conceived child, the Source of Truth will confirm the truth of
the Holy Torah. Through this luminous child, the Source of
Wisdom will transmit the wisdom of the Holy Gospel. My beloved Jesus will declare to the People of Israel: 'Behold, I have
come with wonderful signs from the Source of Love and Power.
As a child I molded from river clay the likeness of a bird. When
I breathed on it, by the mysterious permission of Allah, it became

a white dove that took wing before my mother's eyes. Through me, the Divine Power heals those born blind, cleanses lepers, and reawakens those who have fallen into the sleep of death. I demonstrate the Power of Allah by knowing precisely what people have experienced, what worldly wealth they have stored in their houses, and what spiritual treasure they have hidden within their hearts. These are demonstrations of Love to turn human beings toward the Source of Love. I have come to confirm the Words of Torah that were revealed before me, and also to bring new spiritual freedom. To give the people of Torah confidence in my Prophethood have I come with powerful signs from Allah Most Sublime. By responding wholeheartedly to me, you will be turning toward the Light of Allah. Allah alone is my Source and your Source. The direct path to illumination is to turn your whole life toward the Ever-Present Source.'"

The Resonance of Allah continued to spring forth in the heart of the Virgin Mary: "When the noble Jesus teaches thus, he will be rejected by his people and will cry out: 'Who will help to bear and to transmit the Truth of Allah that is flowing through me?' The blessed apostles will respond: 'Revered teacher, we will be your humble companions and the instruments of Allah Most High, for we have surrendered our lives to the Source of Life. You can witness our submission. We believe wholeheartedly that you are sent as Holy Messenger from the Source and Goal of Being. May our names be inscribed in the Heavenly Book among those who will follow and serve the Messiah Jesus always.'

"After the bitter scheming of those who live in negation of Love has been brought to nothing by the Power of Allah, the Voice of Truth will call these Divine Words into the heart of His holy servant: 'My beloved Jesus, I now draw you back into Me and exalt your being so that you may merge into My Being. I now purify and heal you from the harsh touch of those who deny that you are a messenger from the Source of Love. Be assured that I will transfigure with My Love all those who sincerely follow you, and awakening from the sleep of death, they will experience the radiant resurrection of Paradise. Be assured as well that all souls will eventually return to Me to resolve the conflict and confusion of their earthly journey.'"

—Meditation on *Holy Qur'an* 3:45–55

Mary's Vision of Annunciation

My beloved Muhammad, please recount to your people the awesome visionary experience of the Virgin Mary. Withdrawing at dawn to a solitary room facing east, she contemplated the Source of Beauty during the beautiful desert sunrise. Sitting in deep tranquility, she gradually entered a profound meditative state in which the existence of her family, and even of the whole world, became covered with a veil of Divine Light. On the plane of spiritual vision, more real and more intense than the sphere of mundane perception, My beloved Mary then experienced the conception and birth of the Prophet Jesus.

First the Source of Light manifested to her through an intensely luminous and exalted human form. Startled from her prayerful concentration, she exclaimed: "May the All-Merciful One protect me from this enigmatic being!" The angelic form responded: "Blessed Mary, I am but a servant and messenger of Allah Most High sent to confirm that you will bear a holy child of unsurpassable purity." My beloved one replied: "How can I give birth, having lived in perfect virginity?" The brilliant emissary from the Source of Light explained: "Blessed Virgin Mother, whatever is affirmed by the Source of Being effortlessly comes to be. From before eternity, Allah Most Merciful has ordained this spontaneous childbirth as a unique demonstration of His Love for human beings to contemplate throughout history."

So My beloved Mary, touched then by a ray of Divine Light directly from the Source of Light, instantly conceived, and withdrew in her vision to a secret oasis, remaining secluded there in solitary prayer. Through the mysterious decree of the Source of Power, the holy birth occurred immediately. The contractions overcame her beside the trunk of a palm tree. The baby was delivered swiftly. Shocked and overwhelmed by this miraculous nativity, the holy mother cried out: "Would that I had perished in the desert and that my body had never been found!"

But the newborn babe in her vision spoke soothingly: "My blessed mother Mary, you have no reason to sorrow or to fear. The Source of Love has manifested beside you a spring of fresh water, and if you shake this palm, ripe dates will fall at your feet. So eat, drink, and be comforted in perfect silence by the boundless Mercy of Allah. If you encounter any stranger, exclaim: 'I am fasting in praise of the All-Merciful One and cannot converse with you.'" Still rapt in the higher plane of spiritual vision, she bore home in her arms this child of light. Shocked by the sight of her unwedded motherhood, her family protested: "Daughter of a flawless lineage, none of your ancestors has transgressed the holy way of life. Why have you committed this immoral action?" My beloved one, serene now in her silent submission to the Source of Love, quietly indicated that her family should question the radiant child in her arms. Still more shocked, they cried: "Mary, have you gone mad? How can we converse with a newborn baby?" Thereupon the infant Jesus spoke in sweet, dear tones: "Look carefully. You will see and understand that I am the devoted servant and faithful messenger of Allah Most High. The Source of Wisdom has already placed the Holy Gospel in subtle form within my secret heart and has awakened me as His penultimate Prophet. The Ever-Present Source has emanated me as an utterly blessed human being, no matter where I go or what I undergo. Allah Most Merciful has empowered me to pray unceasingly, and to offer loving service and spiritual illumination to all beings. Most particularly, the Source of Love has taught me to cherish my precious mother, the Virgin Mary, who will be a channel of Divine Love for all future generations. Since my Lord has made me His most humble servant and messenger, the very Peace of Allah Most High will flow through me to all humanity, from the moment of my miraculous birth to the moment of my miraculous ascension into Paradise."

Such was the noble Mary's spiritual vision of the infant Jesus, that pure Messenger of Truth sent forth directly from the Source of Love, whose authentic Prophethood many persons still foolishly dispute. By emanating the exalted prophetic soul of the Messiah Jesus, Allah Most High did not conceive a child in any human sense. This is clearly impossible for the Ultimate Source, Who is simply boundless Radiance. Allah Most Merciful channeled His Word of Love perfectly and immaculately through a living woman of absolute purity. The Source of Being needs only to contemplate the existence of any being and that being comes to be.

My beloved Muhammad, explain to your people: "It is absolutely certain that the Ever-Present Source is your Source no less than my Source. Dedicate your lives completely to the Source of Life. This is the Direct Path of Islam."

—Meditation on *Holy Qur'an* 19:16–36

✿
Friends of Allah

There are truly lovers of Love whose whole being trembles at
the very mention of the Ever-Present Source, Who calls Itself
Allah and Who is completely Love. Whenever the overwhelming demonstrations of Love flowing from Allah Most Sublime
through His Prophets are recounted, these ecstatic souls turn
more and more deeply in pure trust toward the Source of Love.
These are My authentic lovers, whose very lives are lived as praise
and prayer, whose every act is compassionately to share whatever
earthly or heavenly abundance the Ultimate Source has provided
for them. These are the intimate friends of Allah Most High
who experience constantly the healing forgiveness that overflows
from the Source of Love and who, ascending to the higher levels
of realization, regard all events without exception as generous
gifts and teachings from the Source of Wisdom.

—Meditation on *Holy Qur'an* 8:2–4

COMMENTARY:
The Prophet Muhammad

Muhammad's students wrote down the Qur'an after his passing and
compiled the sections into a single piece of sacred literature. Muhammad
originally spoke the individual suras under divine inspiration over many
years during his lifetime. The various suras present guidance given for
specific challenges in the evolution of the early Muslim community as
well as timeless wisdom. The Qur'an presents the Prophet Muhammad
in many different situations, sometimes facing opposition or his own
grief or doubt. Through it all, the voice coming through the Qur'an

guides him to trust the Source of Being and what it is revealing to him.

The "Night of Power" (Sura 97:1–5), translated in this section, is the moment when Muhammad first began to receive the Qur'an. Muslims celebrate this night during Ramadan, the month of daylight fasting.

—*Ed.*

The Sorrow of the Prophet Muhammad

The Ever-Present Source knows intimately your sadness of heart, My beloved, at the bitter words of those who reject this sublime Revelation. There is no lack in you of integrity or compassion. These are simply persons who have brought upon themselves the fatal disease of negation, and who therefore cannot help but feel that any demonstration of Divine Love is imaginary. The Holy Messengers before you were also branded as imposters. With patient and unwavering hearts they accepted this calumny, deeply saddened, until the very Source of Love, Who now manifests through you, flooded them with peace and power. You have no alternative, My beloved Muhammad, but to continue transmitting the Divine Words of this Resonant Qur'an, for no Prophet can change or soften the powerful Message of Truth, and well you know the suffering which, by the Will of Allah, My earlier Messengers had to endure.

—Meditation on *Holy Qur'an* 6:33–4

∝

The Humility of the Prophet Muhammad

The Supreme Source does not awaken Prophets among humanity except to bear the joyous news of homecoming into Paradise,
which is the Radiance of Allah, and to warn of the terrible purification of Hell, which is the very same Divine Radiance. Those
who spontaneously accept the truth of this clear and essential
message, and who respond by struggling to transform every detail of their daily lives into an expression of Love, will never be
overcome by fear or sorrow, and will recognize the overwhelming Splendor of Allah as Paradise. But those who denounce as
mere imagination the Words of Truth that emanate from the
Source of Truth will have to experience the Divine Light as a
fiery chastening to cleanse the disease of their negation.

My beloved Muhammad, humbly inform your people: "I
do not claim to possess any of the boundless Power of Allah
Most High, nor do I claim to perceive what is invisible or to
foretell destiny. Never have I suggested to you that I am some
angelic being. I am simply one who follows carefully what is
revealed to him by the Source of Love."

Proclaim with confidence to your people: "Allah Most Merciful has opened my eyes. Can the knowledge of the blind person
be equal to the knowledge of one who sees? Please meditate upon
this very deeply."

—Meditation on *Holy Qur'an* 6:48–50

⸙

Of Course Not!

The Source of Life, Who weaves the rich tapestry of planetary life, showers sweet rain from beautiful dark clouds, causing the earth to blossom into gardens of surpassing beauty and into rare orchards of delight that no human being could ever bring into Being. Are there any streams of life that do not originate from the Source of Life? Of course not! Yet many persons continue to turn away by elevating cosmic forces to the level of divinity.

The Source of Power establishes the earthly plane of Being as a sanctuary, flowing with great rivers, anchored by primordial mountains, and protected by an intricate natural balance of powers, such as those that keep sea water distinct from fresh water. Is there any power which does not depend upon the Source of Power? Of course not! Yet how few truly embrace this profound understanding.

The Source of Love tenderly responds to the prayers of those who are wronged or threatened by removing oppression and danger, and has appointed human beings to be the sensitive caretakers of this Earth. Is there any response to prayer or call to caring action which originates outside the Source of Love? Of course not! Yet how seldom most persons remember to turn intimately toward their own True Source.

The Source of Wisdom guides humanity across treacherous seas and through uncharted wilderness, sending winds of wise teaching that fill sails and that bear life-giving rain. Is there any wisdom which does not spring forth from the Source of Wisdom? Of course not! But the Ever-Present Source is far beyond any conception or description dreamed of by human beings.

What really is it that continuously brings the universe into

being on higher and higher levels of Being, and eventually returns all manifest Being into the Ultimate Source? What
spontaneously provides every living creature with the subtle nourishment it needs? Is there any being which does not emerge from
the Source of Being? Of course not!

My beloved Muhammad, challenge the thinking of your
people: "Can you present even one authentic demonstration of
another power that exists apart from the Source of Power?" Explain patiently to your people: "No one other than Allah Most
High knows the invisible destiny of any being on the earthly or
heavenly planes of Being. Human beings never know when they
will be called back into the Source and Goal of Being, nor have
they direct knowledge of the sublime nature of Paradise. Yet simply because humanity cannot clearly perceive the realm beyond
death, many foolishly doubt the very existence of such a realm."

—Meditation on *Holy Qur'an* 27:60–6

❧

Alienated Ones

This Glorious Qur'an is the gracefully descending Radiance of
Allah, Who is tender Compassion and Love most sublime. The
eternal Book of Allah has been revealed in the realm of time
through you, My beloved Muhammad, as an Arabic Qur'an, for
all persons who truly seek wisdom. This Living Qur'an transmits My joyous Promise and My merciful Warning, but many
will turn away rather than listen to these Words of Truth with
the inner ear that discerns spiritual meaning.

My beloved, those who fail to listen closely enough will
say to you: "There is an impenetrable veil between our lives and
the way of life to which you are calling us. Your words do not

resound clearly in our hearts. We feel a strange sense of separation from you. Perhaps you should follow your way and leave us to follow our own." This is how you should answer these alienated ones: "My friends, please do not feel that I am a stranger, for I am an ordinary human being, no different from yourselves. I have humbly received anew the ancient revelation that all manifest Being emerges from and returns to the Single Source and Goal of Being, Who refers to Itself as Allah, as well as by countless other most beautiful Divine Names. The essential message that I bear is not strange or obscure, but presents the clear path of consciously turning and returning to the Source. Face Allah alone, opening your hearts to the sweet and healing stream of Divine Forgiveness that flows continuously from the Source of Love. My Divine Warning is directed only to those who interpose limited conceptions between themselves and Allah Most High, to those who do not commit concretely to the service of everyone in need, and to those who fail to trust that the soul awakens from the sleep of death. Those who ceaselessly affirm the Source of Love with their own lives of abundant and overflowing goodness will receive the entire treasure of Divine Love."

—Meditation on *Holy Qur'an* 41:2–8

Coming Home

No human being circumscribed by the limits of creaturely existence can stand directly within the awesome Source of Power, but human beings can communicate and commune with Allah Most High through the mysterious flow of inward inspiration, from behind protective veils of Divine Light, or by association with a Holy Messenger through whom the Ultimate Source can clearly express to humanity whatever It wishes. These creaturely limits are generated because the Perfect Luminous Wisdom, Who is Allah Most High, exists only as Transcendence.

My beloved Muhammad, the Source of Wisdom was first communicated to you, through Its most exalted angelic emanation, when your personal awareness was not yet flooded by the Revelation of the Glorious Arabic Qur'an. The Ever-Present Source awakened you and mysteriously elevated you above the limits of Creation. The Source of Light now shines through you completely as the Light of the Qur'an, by which true servants of Love throughout history will be guided, in mystical companionship with you, directly into the Source of Love.

My noble Messenger, be confident that you are calling humanity along the Direct Path to the Source of Life, Who embraces every life in Heaven and on Earth. To Allah alone are all creatures coming home.

—Meditation on *Holy Qur'an* 42:51–3

Newcomers to Islam

Newcomers to the exalted way of Islam may proclaim: "We have now turned our lives completely toward the Source of Love." Please correct their pride with these Words of Truth: "My friends, do not say that you have turned but that you are still turning, for your hearts have not yet become expressions of Divine Love alone. If you remain loyal to Allah Most High and to the Words of Revelation that flow through His noble Messenger, the Source of Wisdom will gradually deepen your spiritual perception and the Source of Life will enrich you in ways beyond your conception. Allah Most Merciful is boundless Compassion and absolute Forgiveness."

Those whose lives are fully turned to the Source of Love are the ones whose inward loyalty to Allah Most High and to His Messenger of Mercy has been profoundly tested, through the sacrifice to the Ultimate Source of the Universe not only of their worldly wealth but of their entire selves. Those who offer their limited selves in holy sacrifice, without the slightest hesitation or doubt, are the ones who are truly turned toward the limitless Truth.

Newcomers to the noble way of Islam may voice objections. Please correct their pride with these Words of Truth: "Can you teach Allah Most Wise the correct understanding of religion, when Allah alone is the One, Who knows the complete structure and meaning of the heavens and the earth? My friends, please be confident that the Source of Wisdom reveals whatever needs to be revealed."

Another error made by certain beginners, My beloved one, will be to attribute Islam to you rather than to Allah Most High. They will consider it as a favor to you that they have decided to surrender their lives. Please dispel this dangerous distortion with the following admonition: "My friends, never consider your practice of the holy way of life to be a gift to me. What your transformed lives represent is Allah's gift to you, a clear sign of His Loving Guidance. As your spiritual experience becomes more authentic you will realize that you are not turning yourselves toward the Source of Love, but that the Source Itself is turning you. Allah alone knows the invisible destiny of all lives in the heavens and upon the earth. Allah alone knows precisely where you are and who you are."

—Meditation on *Holy Qur'an* 49:14–8

Questioning

My beloved Muhammad, you exist simply to remind humanity of the Ultimate Source, Who speaks through you. You are a perfectly pure vessel of Allah's Own encompassing Awareness, not a shaman who manipulates subtle forces, nor a medium used by wandering and rebellious spirits. Some superficial persons will exclaim about you: "This man is a wonderful poet. Wait and see what strange destiny will be his." Reply to them: "Keep on waiting, my friends. I am waiting also. Moment by moment I wait for the Will of Allah Most High to be revealed, and I live in awe of the onrushing Day of Truth." There are some genuine seekers of truth who will doubt the authenticity of the Holy Qur'an. Will they question because their rational minds are not satisfied? Will they question irrationally, out of sheer arrogance? Will they claim that My Servant and Messenger has merely invented the words of this Glorious Qur'an? No, they will be free from such limited considerations, yet they will remain hesitant to accept the Living Qur'an as pure Divine Revelation. My beloved one, please request these sincere persons to compose verses themselves, or to find verses composed by anyone else, which are comparable in spiritual power to the Divine Words of the Resonant Qur'an. This challenge will test the sincerity of their commitment to truth.

Please confront in this way any persons who approach with sincerity but remain unable to accept wholeheartedly this culmination of Revelation from the Source of Wisdom. "My friends, do you spring into being from nowhere? Do you create yourselves? Do you radiate the entire spectrum of heavenly and earthly existence?" These rhetorical questions will function to awaken such people to their own lack of true inner certitude. "Do you have access to the boundless reservoir of Power? Do you keep precise account of all the lives which flow from the Source of Life? Do you ascend into the Highest Heaven and listen to the conversation of the Archangels?"

Invite those persons who claim to have heard the voices of angels to bring forward some clear confirmation from the Source of Power. As for those who continue to worship mere elemental forces, personified in various forms, ask them: "Do you imagine that the Source of Being conceives minor deities as you procreate children?"

My noble Messenger, please be tireless in questioning those who remain unable to embrace the Revelation flowing through you, and remind them: "My friends, do I require payment for these precious teachings, so that you are forced into debt simply to receive them?" Challenge limited human thinking constantly: "Do you perceive the invisible destiny of the universe and record it in your own Holy Book? Do you aspire to be wiser than the Source of Wisdom? Do you imagine yourselves clever enough to elude or to defraud Allah? Those who turn away from their own True Source are only deluding and defrauding themselves. Do you dream that you can receive revelation from somewhere beyond the One Source?" All the radiance of manifest Being shines only from the Source of Being, Allah Most High, Who is far beyond any human conception or description.

—Meditation on *Holy Qur'an* 52:29–43

⚹

The Call and Enlightenment of the Prophet Muhammad

Cherished humanity, like the evening star that shines more and more brilliantly as night approaches is My beloved Muhammad. This eternal Light of Prophecy and tender companion of all souls is not among those who have been led astray by wandering spirits, nor is he tainted by human error, nor is he speaking from personal initiative. The Luminous Qur'an that descends through him is nothing less than the culmination of Revelation, radiating directly into his secret heart from the Source of awesome Power and clear Wisdom.

The drama of this Revelation was begun by the mysterious angelic emissary who appeared to My beloved Muhammad, first towering above the horizon, then drawing closer until its overwhelming radiance came to rest at the distance of two bows placed end to end, or even nearer. Through this angel of light, the Source of Light revealed to My devoted servant and messenger whatever needed to be revealed as his Call to Prophethood.

The perfectly pure heart and mind of My beloved one could never harbor falsehood. This revelatory event is what he actually experienced. Would anyone be foolish enough to dispute what the Prophet of Allah perceived with his own eyes?

My beloved Muhammad communed with this radiant emissary of Allah Most High at another time, beside the mystic Tree that marks the far boundary of the Highest Heaven. Across this ultimate threshold lies the garden of Essence. The Tree of Life beneath which My Prophet was sitting became engulfed in the mystery of the One Essence. Entering profound meditation, he crossed the final threshold and humbly gazed into the

Essential Light, without turning away even slightly. Thus did My beloved awaken completely into mystic union with the Ever-Present Source.

—Meditation on *Holy Qur'an* 53:1–18

The Transcendent Truth

My beloved Moses cried out to those who contended with him: "My people, why do you argue so bitterly, causing such pain to my heart, when you know that I am a messenger sent to you from the Ultimate Source?" Allah alone allows certain souls to turn from the Words of Revelation that stream through His Messengers. This rejection by some provides testing and teaching for everyone. But until it turns around again toward the Source of Love, no soul that has turned away can receive direct guidance from Allah Most High.

The radiant son of the blessed Virgin Mary, My beloved Jesus, proclaimed to his people: "Children of Israel, I am a messenger from the One Source sent to confirm the Divine Words of the Holy Torah that preceded me and to assure humanity that another such messenger will follow me, whose name will be derived from the word meaning *praise* and whose entire being will shine with the Beauty and Mercy of Allah." When Jesus the Messiah brought the People of Israel clear demonstrations of My Power and My Love, they responded with the charge: "These miracles are mere sorcery." Who can conceive any more serious distortion of the soul than claiming the truth to be falsehood? How can persons suffering such distortion freely respond to the Source of Truth, Who is always calling every soul to the path of constant submission, the way of life which is merged in Divine

Peace? No soul that has turned away, until it turns around again to the Source of Love, can possibly be open to the guidance that streams to all souls from Allah Most High.

Rebellious persons foolishly imagine that they can extinguish the Divine Light with their contentious words. But Allah Most Merciful will continue to reveal the Light of His Mercy, through surrendered human beings, regardless of any obscuration caused by those who turn away from the Source of Light.

Cherished humanity, the Ever-Present Source, Who now reveals the Majestic Name, Allah Most High, has sent the noble Messenger Muhammad to offer authentic guidance along the Way of Truth. Allah has transmitted to His Prophet of Culmination the power to declare the transcendent Truth that extends beyond every religion and yet embraces them all. This Final Revelation will continue to radiate and expand, regardless of any falsehood generated by those who turn away from the Source of Revelation.

—Meditation on *Holy Qur'an* 61:5–9

The Holy Pen

My beloved Muhammad, the instrument of the Universal Intellect, the First Light that radiates eternally from the Source of Light, now inscribes this Living Qur'an in mystic syllables upon the clear pages of your early awareness. My noble Messenger, you are the Holy Pen, and you cannot be used as a channel by any astral or etheric force. Yours is the entire treasure of Knowledge and Love. The Light of Revelation that descends through you is the boundless radiance of Power and Wisdom that streams from the Ultimate Source alone. Humanity will understand your exalted spiritual station with ever increasing clarity, and those who regard you as deluded, mad, or possessed will eventually discover that their own negation of Divine Love is the real insanity.

—Meditation on *Holy Qur'an* 68:1–6

❧ Emissary of Light

My cherished ones, your loving friend and holy companion, My devoted servant Muhammad, is not possessed by some wandering spirit that speaks through him. He encountered instead the supremely exalted Archangel of Allah, who approached him with brilliant clarity from the horizon of Creation. My noble Messenger received through this emissary of light the culmination of Divine Revelation. The Prophet Muhammad is assuredly not a person deceived by arrogance who claims personal knowledge of destiny, the sublime knowledge which belongs only to Allah.

My dear humanity, who is the crown of My Creation, the Living Qur'an is not a communication from some departed soul or some etheric being in rebellion against the Source of Being. Therefore listen with deep trust and reverence to these Words of Truth, and consider carefully where your self-centered way of life is leading you. The Glorious Qur'an is a powerful reminder of Divine Presence, offered by Allah Most Merciful to all Creation, and particularly to those souls who long to return directly to the Source of Love. But such precious spiritual longing cannot well up in the heart of any person except through the Will of Allah Most High, Who is the Cherisher and Sustainer of all worlds.

—Meditation on *Holy Qur'an* 81:22–9

Hardship and Ease

My beloved Muhammad, did not the Source of Love, Who is now speaking, open your secret heart, vastly expanding your conscious being and lifting from you entirely the burden of universal human suffering which weighed down your sensitive awareness as though you carried a huge weight across your shoulders? Did not the Source of Wisdom exalt your entire conscious life into the constant remembrance of Allah Most High? Be assured that with the hardship of rigorous spiritual struggle always comes the sweetness that flows from Allah's Own Delight. With the difficult life of sacrifice for the sake of Allah alone always comes the ease of transcendental bliss. My beloved one, whenever you are free, even for a moment, from the outward responsibility of leadership, continue to labor inwardly at constant prayer, to immerse your being completely in Divine Love. Prayer alone is your life's ultimate purpose.

—Meditation on *Holy Qur'an* 94:1–8

The Inception of the Arabic Qur'an

My beloved Muhammad, thus begins the Arabic Qur'an that will flow powerfully throughout the rest of your lifetime from the Source of Love and Wisdom. You must now recite, and teach humanity to recite, these primordial Divine Words: "Every thought and action springs only from Allah Most High. This is the Majestic Name for the Source and Goal of Being, the Creator and Cherisher of Worlds, the formless Power,

Who evolves every human form from a mere clot of blood."

My beloved, recite as well with the intensity of your entire being this message to humanity from the Ultimate Source, Who speaks through you: "Allah is the All-Merciful One, Who teaches with the mysterious Pen, the Universal Intellect, the instrument of Revelation that inscribes within the secret soul of My servant and messenger this Living Qur'an, unveiling to awakened hearts what is hidden from the eyes of mundane understanding."

—Meditation on *Holy Qur'an* 96:1–5

The Night of Power

My noble Messenger, please teach humanity to celebrate with awe the first moment that the Source of Light began to radiate Its Luminous Qur'an through your earthly being. This is the moment during your solitary mountain retreat when you plunged into Divine Mystery on the Night of Power, and your personal awareness first received the resplendent Words of Allah.

It is impossible to conceive the true import of this Night of Power, which is mystically manifest each year, sometime during the most holy month of Ramadan, on the hidden anniversary of your awakening to the Radiant Qur'an. To enter spiritually into the shining realm of this Night of Nights is more powerful than practicing intense prayer for one thousand months. During this transcendent Night, by the permission of Allah, angelic beings descend freely into human hearts in response to every prayerful longing. Within the unfathomable mystery of this Night, Allah's Own Light can be received directly by souls who are immersed in the ecstasy of true contemplation. The perfect Peace of the eternal Source descends completely into the Creation during the Night of Power. This miraculous transformation of the universe into Paradise remains until the first glow of dawn.

—Meditation on *Holy Qur'an* 97:1–5

⚭

The Way of Islam

My noble Messenger, respond to those who have decisively turned away from the Source and Goal for Being: "You who negate the Source of Being, and thereby the very Ground of your own being, cannot revere the One Whom I revere, nor can I exalt what you exalt. I cannot offer my life to the self-centered goals that you perceive, nor can you offer your lives to the encompassing Goal that I perceive, because you have turned away from the Source of Life. Yours is the way of limited human intelligence, mine the limitless way of Islam.

—Meditation on *Holy Qur'an* 109:1–6

COMMENTARY
The Qur'an

The Qur'an describes its own voice as something that goes beyond the utterance of any individual prophet. Its unique expression comes through the Arabic of the 7th century, and yet the individual words convey more than meaning or theology. Muslims hear and feel the rhythm, tone, cadence, feeling, and atmosphere of the Qur'an as the voice of the One Being, who paradoxically says that it is beyond any personification or humanly conceivable personality. On an even more profound level, the Qur'an says that it is only one *particular* expression of an uncreated or, as Lex Hixon translates it, Transcendent Qur'an.

This archetypal "text," which is beyond all human words and also called the "Mother of the Book," is the source of all holy books of all times and traditions. The Qur'an also repeatedly speaks against the habitual human tendency to need a "miracle" in order to be reminded of the One Reality. As it says in the selection from Sura 6 below, all of manifestation is a living miracle in action, and the Qur'an itself is a miracle—both a specific teaching for a particular people as well as the expression of the uncreated and eternal voice of the Ground of Being.

—*Ed.*

Living Guidance

The Living Truth alone flows through these Arabic letters and imbues each with mystic potency. This is the Book of Truth, clear from every doubt, that guides the steps of those who turn their entire lives toward Allah, the Source of Truth, and who always feel surrounded by the invisible Divine Presence. This Living Qur'an guides those who plunge wholeheartedly into prayer and who freely share whatever earthly abundance the Ever-Present Source provides for them. This Radiant Qur'an guides those who accept with reverence the Divine Words transmitted through you, My beloved Muhammad, and the Words of Truth sent from the Ultimate Source through the Prophets before you. This Resonant Qur'an guides those who experience certitude that after the sleep of death they will awaken into the Radiance of Allah. These are the truly human beings who can consciously receive Living Guidance from Allah Most High, and whose earthly lives on every level become fruitful. As for those who suffer the delusion of negation and who finally come to deny the very Ground of their own being, it makes no difference whether you warn them or not. They have turned away entirely from the Source of Life. To protect them from being utterly consumed by their own negativity, Allah Most Merciful has sealed their secret hearts, silenced their spiritual hearing, and veiled their inner vision. Entering into the sleep of death, they will experience the beauty of Divine Resplendence as a terrible purification by fire.

—Meditation on *Holy Qur'an* 2:1–7

∽

Miracles

Allah Most Sublime is worthy of the endless praise of all beings. Allah alone has emanated the temporal universe and the eternal planes of Being. From Allah alone radiates the Light of Truth, and upon this Light alone even the shadows of error depend. Yet human beings continue to reject the holy way of life by failing to rely on the limitless Source, placing their reliance instead on various limited forces and concepts. The Power of Allah alone has shaped the human species from substances of earth, determining with complete wisdom the scope of each personal life, the lives of civilizations, and the life span of the entire universe. Yet human beings continue to doubt, openly or secretly within themselves, the profound significance of all existence.

Allah Most High is just as present to His planetary realm as He is to His heavenly realm. As encompassing Awareness, Allah knows intimately from before eternity the thoughts and deeds, secret and open, of every being. Thus Allah knows precisely what level of goodness and understanding each soul will attain through the sincere struggle and subtle experience of an entire lifetime. Yet whenever clear reminders of this embracing

Divine Awareness are sent through the noble Prophets, many people still turn away, claiming the precious Words of Revelation to be myth or imagination. But those who ignore, deny, or even deride the truth that Allah Most Merciful reveals repeatedly to humanity, will eventually encounter the Living Truth directly.

In the course of history, when civilizations turn away from the harmonious life of conscious submission to the Source of Life, they deteriorate and are eventually destroyed. Consider how many powerful nations the Supreme Source has allowed to disappear from the earth, washed away by the torrent of time, nations much more firmly established and blessed with abundance than your people, My beloved Muhammad. The Source of Life invigorated these ancient nations with the Water of Life, but later generations were swept aside because their way of life had lost its purity and resilience by ignoring and even negating the Source of Life. In place of these lifeless civilizations, Allah Most Merciful nourishes new peoples who turn wholeheartedly toward their own True Source.

My beloved, the most astonishing miracles could not help you to draw to the Source of Love those who are consumed by their own negation of Love. Even were the Ultimate Source to send this Holy Qur'an from the sky, written on heavenly parchment, so that people could touch Revelation with their own hands, those turned away from Love would proclaim: "This is the work of a powerful sorcerer." Other chronic doubters cry: "Why was no angelic being sent down to appear beside the Prophet for all to see?" Had the Ever-Present Source revealed to mundane vision the angels of light that surround My noble Messenger, faith would be divinely imposed authority rather than free human response. Had Allah Most High sent His Archangel in place of My devoted servant Muhammad, the sublime human relationship to the Source of Love would never have been dramatized and clarified.

—Meditation on *Holy Qur'an* 6:1–9

∽

Words of Truth

The Source of Wisdom now reveals a parable for profound contemplation. Words of Truth that have the power to express the Living Truth are like flourishing trees whose roots, or direct meanings, are established deep in the earth of the heart and whose branches, or subtle meanings, reach high into the sky of mystical knowledge. By the mysterious permission of Allah, these trees bear fruit during every season. Merely human words, by contrast, are like dry trees rooted in shallow, sandy soil, which are easily brought down by the relentless winds of error, having no firm grounding in the secret heart. Through such parables, My beloved, the Source of Light illuminates the nature of this Glorious Qur'an so that humanity may meditate and truly understand.

Allah Most Merciful blesses those whose lives are turned toward the Source of Love with the life-giving Divine Words of the Holy Qur'an, vast trees of meaning that provide refreshing shade and nourishing fruit, both during earthly existence and within the timeless realm of Paradise. Those who turn away from the Source of Love have access only to fleeting words, merely human expressions with no abiding life in the Truth. Grasping at these dry, lifeless words, such persons appear to wander farther and farther from Allah Most High. Yet no being can actually move the slightest distance from the Ever-Present Source of Being. The merciful Will of Allah is beyond any comprehension.

—Meditation on *Holy Qur'an* 14:24–7

⚭

The Descent of the Holy Qur'an

The Supreme Source radiates the Truth-bearing Qur'an through the seven subtle realms. Gracefully this Book of Light descends, full of Divine Power and Beauty, into your most pure and receptive being, My beloved Muhammad. The Source of Love has chosen you from before eternity to become the final reservoir of My Revelation, to bear the Living Qur'an that conveys joyous news about the Radiance of Paradise and compassionate warning that this very Radiance may be experienced as the fire of Hell.

My beloved Messenger, the Source of Wisdom now manifests the perfect wholeness of the Eternal Qur'an through the temporal veils of human experience, revealing the Divine Words to you at intervals to create an earthly book, clothed in the Arabic language, that will be comprehensible to humanity. This is why the Ever-Present Source sends the Transcendent Qur'an to you gradually, rather than flooding your awareness in an instant with its totality. Say to your people: "Either believe in the authenticity of these Divine Words, whenever they come, or believe not."

Certain souls enjoy most intimate acquaintance with the Eternal Qur'an before they descend into time, and when these persons hear even one line of the present Arabic Qur'an, they fall to the earth in ecstatic recognition, proclaiming: "These very words are the Resonance and Radiance of Allah. The original promise of Allah Most Merciful to guide humanity has once again been fulfilled." These lovers of Divine Love, upon hearing the chanting of the Arabic Qur'an, will spontaneously place their foreheads on the sanctified earth, shedding tears and experiencing the profound humility that completely forgets the limited self.

My beloved, please assure your people that in gentle and

harmonious tones they can invoke the Ultimate Source with the
Name of Majesty, Allah Most High, or as the Most Merciful
One, or with any of the beautiful Divine Names presented
through the Prophets to humanity.

—Meditation on *Holy Qur'an* 17:105–10

The Sublime Sanctuary

My beloved Muhammad, to those who doubt the authenticity
of the Holy Qur'an, or the Holy Torah that preceded it, present
this test of sincerity: "If you are really concerned with truth,
then seek out another Book of Revelation that flows more clearly
from the Source of Wisdom, and dedicate your lives to those
teachings." If those who doubt you find no response to this pro-
posal, they are just doubting for the sake of doubting. The most
dangerous illusion is to follow subjective impulses, such as doubt,
while ignoring the guidance of Allah Most Merciful that streams
abundantly through His noble Messengers. Yet this precious Living Guidance cannot be recognized or received by those who
have heedlessly turned away from the Source of Guidance.

Through you, My beloved, the Ever-Present Source, Who
is now speaking, has once more offered Words of Truth to humanity, awakening again the life-giving remembrance of Allah
Most High. There are certain souls who have already received
from the Source of Love mystical intimations of this Resonant
and Radiant Qur'an. When My Divine Words are first chanted
in their presence, these souls of Love spontaneously exclaim: "We
trust this Revelation implicitly. Without any doubt, this is the
Living Truth, radiating directly from the Source of Truth. Even
before hearing these incomparable Words of Power, we had

already surrendered our entire being to their Source." These servants of Love will receive more blessings than anyone can imagine for the suffering they patiently endure as they meet hostility and aggression with sheer goodness of heart, and as they constantly share with others whatever wealth the Source of Abundance has provided for them. Whenever the lovers of Divine Love encounter foolish or even derisive remarks, they turn aside calmly with these gracious words: "We are dedicated to our way of life, and you to yours. May the Peace of Allah Most High be with you. We could not bear your mode of existence that ignores the Source of Existence."

My beloved one, you know that you are not guiding the persons whom you choose but that the Source of Light guides through you the persons whom Allah chooses. The Source of Wisdom alone knows precisely which beings are open to the highest wisdom.

Certain pragmatic persons will confront you in this way: "Were we to follow completely the path of this guidance which you appear to receive from Allah, we would soon lose our lands and all the belongings we have accumulated." These are the hypocritical ones who, when attempting to please Allah Most High, are really seeking to please themselves. Such narrowly calculating minds cannot understand that the Ultimate Source has established through My beloved Servant and Messenger a sanctuary of absolute spiritual protection, where the finest fruits of life have been gathered as a gift to humanity from the Source of Love. How few human beings consciously enter this sublime sanctuary.

—Meditation on *Holy Qur'an* 28:49–57

Spider Webs

Those who seek protection and guidance by contacting various forces on the subtle planes of existence, thereby turning the face of their being away from the Source of Being, are weaving spider webs of etheric energy and attempting to take refuge there. The floating abode of the spider is the most vulnerable of dwelling places. Those who rely for strength on the gossamer web of relative structures and experiences should meditate on its insubstantiality. Allah Most High knows instantly when any being places the slightest spiritual reliance on any limited power or conception, for Allah is boundless and encompassing Awareness.

My beloved, the Source of Wisdom sends these living parables through you to illumine humanity, but no one can understand them profoundly who has not received the Divine Gift of mystical interpretation.

The full spectrum of heavenly and earthly realms radiates from the Source of Truth as the pure and harmonious expression of Truth. Therefore every being and every event present subtle teachings to those who are turned consciously toward their own True Source.

—Meditation on *Holy Qur'an* 29:41–4

The Constant Touch

The person whose innermost heart has been opened by the Source of Love and whose whole being has been expanded to embrace the holy way of Islam shines as a clear ray of light from the Source of Light. But those who allow their hearts and minds to close and harden against the constant touch of Divine Presence wander through the obscure chaos of impulse and error.

My beloved, through you the Source of Wisdom radiates these most beautiful teachings as the coherent tapestry of the Living Qur'an that interweaves Divine Warning and Divine Promise. When this Resonant Qur'an is chanted, those wholly in awe of Allah Most High will feel their bodies trembling subtly. Not just the spiritual heart but the entire being, including every pore of the skin, will become sensitive to the constant touch of Divine Presence. Such delicate sensitivity alone can receive direct guidance from the Source of Love, an experience that cannot be attained by effort but that arises mysteriously through the Will of Allah alone. Those whom Allah Most Wise allows the illusion of wandering away from the Ever-Present Source cannot experience this direct and vibrant sense of the Divine Embrace.

—Meditation on *Holy Qur'an* 39:22–3

Clarity

This Luminous Qur'an is a Book of Divine Clarity sent down through you, My beloved Muhammad, beginning on the most blessed night of your mystical awakening. Within this Radiant Qur'an, which first began to permeate your awareness on that holy Night of Power, are contained countless wise instructions that emanate directly from the Source of Wisdom. The Ever-Present Source has continuously sent clear teaching and guidance to humanity. Revelation is the spontaneously overflowing Mercy of Allah Most High, Who hears and knows the secret longing of all hearts for the Truth. For human beings who awaken to their own true longing and who turn trustingly toward the Source of Light, Divine Presence is clearly revealed, brilliantly pervading the heavens and the earth, creating, filling, and illuminating every space imaginable. There is no source other than the Ultimate Source, Who alone grants life and Who withdraws each life again into the Source of Life. My beloved one, this Single Source is your most precious Allah, precisely the same True Source toward Whom spiritually awakened human beings have turned since the beginning of time.

—Meditation on *Holy Qur'an* 44:2–8

All Is Written

My beloved Muhammad, please teach your people that human life when turned away from the Source of Love is only a game, a diversion, an empty ritual, a chaos of arrogance and conflict over personal power and possession. Here is a parable for deep contemplation: Worldly existence without devotion to the Source of Existence is a brief rain that turns the land just green enough to satisfy those who seek their own immediate pleasure. Very soon this green begins to yellow, and their selfish way of life dries up like straw right before their eyes.

Plunging into the sleep of death, souls either dream in delirium about the terrible fire of purification or awaken with tranquility into the sweet forgiveness and overwhelming bliss of Paradise. Please assure humanity that the surface pleasures of selfish existence are empty imaginings when compared to the profound joy of life in the depth of Divine Existence, the full participation in Divine Life called Paradise. Encourage devoutly loving souls to race with utter abandon into the All-Forgiving Source of Love, where they will enter through spiritual vision a mystic garden more vast than universal space and the seven heavenly realms. This garden of Divine Delight has been opened for those whose lives affirm Truth and who accept wholeheartedly the radiant Messengers of Truth as rays shining from the Single Source into every nation throughout history. Such is the unimaginable Generosity of Allah, poured out for whomever He chooses. The very nature of the Ever-Present Source is to overflow with gifts of goodness beyond any conception or description.

My beloved one, please enlighten your people with this most profound teaching. No suffering occurs in the outer world or in their own hearts that is not already inscribed in the Transcendent Qur'an before the Source of Being brings any event into Being. The miraculous process of unfolding eternal Awareness through temporal experience, to test and to teach the soul, is absolutely effortless for the Ultimate Source, Who is now speaking. Please inspire humanity to meditate on the truth that all is written. Persons will then cease to grieve over what they imagine might have been, or to rejoice over what they imagine has been brought about by their own efforts. The Source of Love cannot flood with Divine Love those who have veiled their own hearts with coarse arrogance or with subtle pride. The surest way to turn away from the Source of Love is to claim responsibility for what comes about purely by the Will of Allah Most Merciful, stimulating others as well to live in this negation of fundamental human gratitude. Although many persons thus willfully turn away, Allah Most High, Who needs absolutely nothing, remains the Only Recipient of the spontaneous praise that arises, consciously or not, from every mind and heart in His Creation.

—Meditation on *Holy Qur'an* 57:20–4

The Central Vein

My beloved, swear to your people by all they can see and by the endless dimensions that are invisible to them that this Radiant and Resonant Qur'an is spoken through an authentic Messenger of Allah. My Living Qur'an could never be the eloquent speech of a poet, words expressing only human power and beauty, although persons of small spiritual capacity will believe this Book of Truth to be poetry. Still less could My Glorious Qur'an be the speech of a shaman, who manipulates elemental and etheric forces, although persons of limited spiritual vision will not appreciate this distinction. Please assure humanity that the Holy Qur'an descends directly as clear Revelation from the Ultimate Source and Goal of the Universe.

My dear human beings, were the blessed and noble Prophet Muhammad merely to invent from his own mind any words he then attributed to Allah Most High, the Source of Power would grasp him by the right hand and open his body's central vein. Not even the most loyal lovers and companions could then prevent his precious lifeblood from flowing away. Know with complete conviction and certitude that the Holy Qur'an is an authentic reminder spoken directly by Allah Most High for those who turn with purity of heart toward their own True Source alone. Allah is fully aware that certain human beings will reject His Reminder and that those who negate the Source of Love will create intense suffering for themselves. The only concern and the only true task for those who accept this Divine Reminder is to live lives of prayer and to praise the beautiful Names of Allah, Who is limitless Glory and absolute Transcendence.

—Meditation on *Holy Qur'an* 69:38–51

Constant Remembrance

What strange obsession plagues human beings, causing them to turn away from the clear reminder that you bring, My beloved, as frightened as wild asses fleeing the mountain lion? These fearful ones excuse themselves for turning away by complaining that the Holy Qur'an did not manifest miraculously, already inscribed on heavenly scrolls. Such hypocrites actually feel no genuine reverence toward Allah Most High and fail entirely to sense the awesome implication of the onrushing Day of Truth. Do not make these people your concern. This Glorious Qur'an is a reminder for those who can respond intuitively and spontaneously, and they will be elevated into continuous communion with their own True Source. No one can attain the high spiritual station of constant remembrance unless it is bestowed as pure Divine Gift from the eternally overflowing fountain of magnificent Power and tender Mercy.

—Meditation on *Holy Qur'an* 74:49–56

The Hidden Illumination of the Holy Qur'an

My beloved Muhammad, has not the Ultimate Source transmitted through you the history of Pharaoh and Thamood, whose vast armies were decimated by My Divine Power? Disregarding these perfectly clear teachings, those among your people who negate the Source of Wisdom foolishly continue to do battle against My Glorious Qur'an, claiming this culmination and reservoir of all the Divine Revelation that has descended throughout time to be mere human imagination. Were these persons simply to turn around, they would know that the Source of Power is behind them, and that It encompasses them from every direction and dimension of Being. My noble Messenger, these Words of Truth that you bear for all humanity are indeed the Book of Light, the Radiant Qur'an, but their illumination is kept subtly hidden, well guarded from mundane vision.

—Meditation on *Holy Qur'an* 85:17–22

⸙

Spring Rain

This Luminous and Living Qur'an, as constant in its patterns as the movement of constellations, is like the abundant rain returning every springtime, causing the fertile soil of the human heart to burst forth again with greenness. These Words of Truth bear the full power of Divine Revelation. They are not the mere play of creative imagination.

—Meditation on *Holy Qur'an* 86:11–4

Chapter Six

A WAY OF LIVING

COMMENTARY
Prayer

In addition to speaking about the nature of ultimate reality and of revelation, the Qur'an offers human beings a way of living. The "five pillars" of Islam—profession of faith (*shahada*), prayer (*salat*), giving to charity (*zakat*), fasting during the month of Ramadan (*sawm*), and pilgrimage (*hajj*)—all have inner and outer dimensions as described by the Qur'an.

Prayer in Islam is not merely a matter of saying particular words at particular times. The attitude of praise leads one to the threshold of the wordless reality of Allah, such that one can also see prayer as the uninterrupted contemplation of the One Being. Purification before prayer (ablution or *wudu*) happens not only outside, but also inside as one strives to keep one's thoughts and emotions centered on Allah. Likewise the direction in which Muslims pray, toward the Ka'bah in Mecca, represents not only a physical place, but also the heart of Allah, which ultimately is found within the heart of one's own, and every, being.

—*Ed.*

❧

The Prayer of the Prophet Muhammad

My beloved Messenger, please teach human beings aspiring to true humanity to pray: "Most exalted Allah, Ruler of the radiant expanse of earthly and heavenly realms, You reveal the potent secrets of Your kingdom to whomever You will, and veil them from whomever You will. As pure Divine Mystery, You elevate whomever You will and limit whomever You will. Your Hands of Power and Goodness hold whatever is needed for the development of each living being, shaping as sensitive spiritual teaching every personal and every cosmic event, for through You alone all events become possible. You alone cause the night of ignorance to disappear into the day of knowledge, and the day of human knowledge, in turn, to disappear into the night of Divine Mystery. You alone cause the living to enter the sleep of death, and You alone awaken those who have died into Your Own transcendent Life. Most precious Allah, Your constant provision for the evolution of all beings is subtle beyond any understanding."

—Meditation on *Holy Qur'an* 3:26–7

❧

Ablution

Cherished lovers of Allah, while you purify your hearts before plunging into the profound prayers of Islam, purify your bodies as well. The precious human body is the vehicle that bowing, kneeling, and prostrating, will carry you deep into Divine Resplendence. Rinse with clear water your hands, mouth, arms, face, head, and feet. Performed while repeating the Majestic Name of Allah, these simple gestures become a purification of the whole being from negativity and distortion. This is true preparation for prayer, not just washing after the natural acts of elimination and passion. This healing, refreshing, and transforming ablution comes from the Power of Allah, not from the touch of water. If you are sick, or traveling, or water is not available, simply wipe your face and hands with clean dust from the earth while repeating My Holy Name. This practice of ablution has not been revealed by the Source of Wisdom to add difficulty to the performance of prayers, but because Allah Most High wishes to purify and exalt the entire being of His lovers so they may merge into His Being. Experiencing daily this spiritual transformation, the lovers of Love are always flooded with gratitude. At every moment they remember the gift of return to the Source of Love conferred on those who have assimilated with their whole being the commands of Allah. They repeat fervently with each breath: "We hear and we obey." My dear human beings who aspire to be truly human, turn with awe toward the Ultimate Source. The encompassing Awareness, Who calls Itself Allah, already knows the secret thoughts and longings of every mind and heart.

—Meditation on *Holy Qur'an* 5:7–8

Praise

Whatever human beings say about reality, whatever advanced concepts they may hold, the Ultimate Source, Who is now speaking, will always be more exalted. All that is possible for any being is to praise Allah Most High, for none can describe Him. The very nature and function of Being itself is to praise the Source and Goal of Being. The entire temporal universe, as well as the seven eternal realms and all the forms of consciousness they contain, are simply the living praise of the Ever-Present Source. To be is to praise Allah. Human beings fail to perceive this boundless praise arising spontaneously from all minds and hearts, or else they would understand instantly why such utter compassion and forgiveness flow to every being from the Source of Love.

—Meditation on *Holy Qur'an* 17:43–4

Daily Prayers

My noble Messenger, please remind your people to plunge into prayer during the delicate glow of twilight, when the sun disappears below the horizon, and again when the evening light blends into the rich blackness of night, and again during the fresh clarity of dawn. The quality of light at each divinely ordained time of prayer is the expression of a certain sphere of spiritual experience. During the clear light before sunrise, angelic beings are present, enjoying the sweet sounds of the Resonant Qur'an and witnessing the pure intentions of the heart at the day's beginning. Those who wish to enter most profoundly into prayer should perform their humble prostrations during the deep night when, by the Will of Allah Most High, the light of human knowledge disappears into the glowing darkness of Divine Mystery. Through this solitary midnight meditation, Allah Most Merciful may choose to elevate the devout soul to a rare state of mystical illumination.

Please teach dedicated persons these Words of Truth with which to concentrate their entire minds on the Source of Truth: "Most exalted Allah, as each breath is drawn in, lead me inward with purity and strength to Your invisible Life, and as each breath flows out, lead me outward with purity and strength to Your manifest Creation. Most precious Allah, please grant me Your Direct Guidance along the subtle way of awakening."

My beloved, convey to lovers of Truth who have been properly prepared the potent words of this sublime affirmation: "The Living Truth now shines completely and all error has vanished utterly, for where the Light of Allah is, no veil of darkness can remain."
—Meditation on *Holy Qur'an* 17:78–81

Pure Peace

My cherished ones who have completely oriented your lives to the Source of Life, remain immersed always in the silent remembrance of Allah Most High. During the prayers at dawn and dusk, pour forth from your lips the most sweet and glorious praises. It is the One Source Who blesses you with the inward experience of bliss, sometimes touching you through luminous angelic beings to guide you from the shadows of the limited self into the Clear Light of the Source. Those who turn constantly toward their own True Source experience the Ever-Present Source as the most delicate Mercy and the most tender Love. Awakening from the sleep of death into the infinite Day of Truth, these souls will be greeted intimately by Allah Most Merciful with the supreme salutation: "May you abide in My Peace." With boundless generosity, the Source of Peace receives these dedicated souls into Its Own pure Peace.
—Meditation on *Holy Qur'an* 33:41–4

∝

The Prayer of Love

The most intimate friends of Allah Most High actually bear His Throne mystically upon their shoulders of silent meditation. Somewhat less rare among human souls are the ecstatic lovers of Allah Most Beautiful, who chant melodiously and move gracefully around the Throne of Essence, lost entirely in the action of perfect praise. These lovers of Love affirm the Source of Love with every breath, and for the protection and illumination of all persons who are striving to turn their lives toward the Ultimate Source, the true lovers pray ceaselessly the prayer of Love:

"Most precious Allah, as tender Mercy and encompassing Awareness, You embrace every life. May those who repent their negation of Love consciously experience Your absolute Forgiveness. May they receive constant encouragement to walk Your most exalted way of Islam, and thereby be spared Your awesome Divine Chastening. Most merciful Allah, please bring all souls home into the Source of Love, which they will experience as gardens of Eden, radiant and timeless. This has been Your Eternal Promise to those who become immersed in goodness and who transmit goodness by embracing with love the parents, spouses, children, and friends with whom their pure hearts are inextricably joined. Most exalted Allah, You alone are boundless Power and complete Wisdom. Please prevent aspiring souls from falling back subtly into negation, for through the protection and guidance of Allah alone can any soul stand free from negativity on the Day of Truth." Those who pray spontaneously in this way have consciously received the fullness of My Mercy, and theirs is the most glorious victory.

—Meditation on *Holy Qur'an* 40:7–9

❧

Inquire Inwardly

My noble Messenger, please offer humanity these potent spiritual instructions: "My friends, have you thought deeply about your existence? As you prepare the soil for sowing, inquire inwardly whether it is really you who scatter the seeds, or whether they are sown through you by the Source of Life. If Allah Most High wished to test you, the Source of Power could reduce fertile soil to dry powder, leaving you to lament: 'Now we will plunge into debt and be deprived of every comfort.' My friends, have you thought deeply about your existence? As you are refreshed by drinking cool water, inquire inwardly whether you bring it down from the beautiful dark clouds, or whether the Source of Life showers this essential blessing upon the earth. If Allah Most High wished to chasten you, the Source of Power could cause bitter rain to fall. Even for the simplest gifts of life you should feel profound gratitude toward the Source of Life. As you kindle the cooking fire, inquire inwardly whether you planted the trees and made them grow, or whether the vast forests on this planet are not really nurtured by the Source of Life alone. Allah Most Merciful sustains every detail of existence, providing firewood and fire as precious gifts for those who dwell in the wilderness, reminding them constantly of the Source of Love. My friends, chant melodiously and cherish with every breath the Majestic Name for the Ultimate Source of the Universe, Allah All-Powerful."

As surely as the stars will fall from the sky at the end of time—and who can know the awesomeness of this Divine Promise?—just as surely is My Living Qur'an utterly noble and sublime. This Revelation is a mysteriously veiled Book of Light, descending directly from the Source of Light, containing Words of Truth whose secret meanings cannot be touched except with minds and hearts completely purified by Allah Most High.

—Meditation on *Holy Qur'an* 56:63–80

Friday Prayer

My dear human beings who aspire to turn your lives completely toward the Source of Love, the moment you hear the midday call to prayer on Friday, drop every concern and enter joyfully together the mosque of Allah's Very Presence. This potent time of gathering, the holy day of congregation, mystically reflects the eternal Day. Were you to glimpse the spiritual mystery of this weekly event, not even the slightest social or personal consideration could deflect your loving concentration at that hour.

When the Friday Prayer of perfect harmony is completed, go forth entirely refreshed and renewed into the radiant Creation of Allah Most High, to seek and receive abundant gifts from the Source of Abundance. Yet during even the most intense experience within the arena of action, learn to sustain a flow of constant inward remembrance of the Ever-Present Source. Those who live their lives as praise of Allah will be blessed and elevated in every way.

My beloved Muhammad, when persons are drawn away from the blessing of your companionship by the distractions of the world, leaving you standing quietly alone, call out to them: "Please remember, my people, that nearness to the Prophet of Love and intimacy with the Source of Love are far sweeter and more valuable than diversion or commerce. Allah alone is the Source of Delight and the Source of Abundance."

—Meditation on *Holy Qur'an* 62:9–11

Vigil

My beloved Muhammad, please instruct those who experience genuine spiritual longing to cover their heads with their shawls and meditate in solitary vigil throughout the night, save for a few hours of light sleep. To counteract drowsiness, My Resonant Qur'an should be chanted distinctly, with intense mindfulness of its inner significance. When this meditative practice is faithfully performed, the Source of Light will shine into the soul of the contemplative through the Divine Words of My Radiant Qur'an as progressively richer and more sublime levels of spiritual meaning. This practice of awakening for meditation at the peaceful midnight hour intensifies both spoken prayer and silent praise. One should return to sleep during the hours before dawn, for daily responsibilities are long and demanding. Yet throughout the day, the contemplative repeats softly or silently with every breath the beautiful Names of the Supreme Source, and with deep devotion consciously dedicates all thought and action to Allah alone.

Allah Most High is forever the same Ever-Present Source, whether in the farthest regions of the East or the West, for there can be only one Ultimate Source. So encourage humanity to turn toward the Source of Power alone for protection. And bear patiently any cruel or foolish words spoken in response to My Message, taking leave of these people with dignity and kindness. Allah alone can purity those who, intoxicated by selfish enjoyments, vehemently reject your counsel to turn their lives toward the Source of Love. For these souls, whose superficial pleasures may continue for a few more years, there eventually awaits the awesome Divine Chastening. Plunging into the sleep of death, they will dream with images drawn from their own negation of Love. Their excruciating experience of fiery bonds and food that burns will reflect the negativity these souls inflicted on others during their earthly existence. These dreadful dreams of purification, ordained by Allah Most Merciful, will begin at the precise moment of physical death, when the entire landscape of their awareness will quake as these souls who have lived in negation of Love desperately try to climb up steep mountains which have become sliding sand.

—Meditation on *Holy Qur'an* 73:1–14

Training for the Soul

After humbly taking ablution while repeating the Majestic Name of Allah Most High, the person who plunges wholeheartedly into prayer will certainly discover the treasure of Love. But human beings cannot easily accept the simplicity of this holy way, preferring to wander instead through the complex distractions and ambitions of mundane existence.

Earthly life is an austere period of training, precious preparation for the soul's enduring experience of the Bliss and Radiance of Allah called Paradise. This fundamental insight shines forth from all the ancient scriptures and is revealed with illuminating clarity in the noble prophetic lineage of My beloved Abraham and My beloved Moses.

—Meditation on *Holy Qur'an* 87:14–9

∞

Abundance

My beloved Muhammad, the Ever-Present Source has revealed within you the eternally flowing fountain of complete spiritual abundance. This is why you live your life spontaneously in prayer to Allah alone, offering every breath as conscious praise and every action as holy sacrifice. Whoever hates or thoughtlessly rejects you, My beloved, is turning away from Allah Most Sublime, and will experience the bitter delusion of hopelessness, which is separation from the Source of Love.

—Meditation on *Holy Qur'an* 108:1–3

∞

Constant Help

My cherished human beings, when you begin consciously to experience the constant help that flows from the Source of Power, victory is near in your struggle to become truly human. You will then perceive many of those around you gratefully entering the exalted way of Islam, which is the surrender and release of narrow individual life into the boundless Source of Life. This universal dawning of gratitude will be a sign to deepen and to intensify your praise of the Ultimate Source, praying intensely that all humanity without exception may receive consciously the sweet forgiveness that flows freely from the Source of Love. Again and again, Allah Most High turns mercifully toward human beings, flooding every mind and heart in His Creation with Living Presence and Divine Light.

—Meditation on *Holy Qur'an* 110:1–3

❦

The Dawn of Love

My beloved Muhammad, please instruct and inspire humanity to take refuge in Allah Most High with this potent prayer: "May I lose myself in the Source of Love, Who abides in all hearts as the eternal dawn of love. May I be protected by Allah Most Powerful against those who turn away from their own True Source, and against the darkness and confusion which they generate. May I be protected by Allah Most Powerful against all projections of negative energy, from the casting of harmful spells to the bitter hatred of those who are consumed by envy."

—Meditation on *Holy Qur'an* 113:1–5

❦

True Refuge

My beloved Muhammad, please teach devoted souls this powerful spiritual affirmation: "I take refuge in Allah alone, the Supreme Guide of humanity. I take refuge in Allah alone, the Mysterious King of humanity. I take refuge in Allah alone, the True Source of humanity."

My noble Messenger, present the precious way of refuge with these potent Words of Truth: "From the self-deceiving whisper of arrogance that distorts the hearts and minds of human beings, and of beings who dwell on subtle planes, the Source of Love alone can provide true refuge."

—Meditation on *Holy Qur'an* 114:1–6

COMMENTARY
Gratitude and Giving

The Arabic word *zakat* (charity) originally meant "virtue," to be pure or acquitted from any wrongdoing. Specifically, the Qur'an sees piling up possessions for oneself as a burden on the spiritual path, and so giving away what one does not need helps one stay closer to the divine. After the Prophet and his followers were forced to move to Medina, more people flocked to Islam and some were very poor. At this time, the voice of the Qur'an instituted the formal practice of giving alms to charity. This practice has varied widely in different Muslim countries over the centuries. Yet the underlying emphasis of the Qur'an remains clear: gratitude and giving help free the soul.

—Ed.

Giving

My beloved Muhammad, please warn human beings never to imagine any divinity other than the Ultimate Source of the Universe, for such imagination will defraud and disgrace them by veiling the One Ever-Present Source. Allah Most Merciful has clearly taught human beings to turn in worship solely and directly towards the Source of Love, transforming their entire lives into perfect expressions of Divine Love.

My cherished human souls, be tender to your parents, particularly when father and mother, while residing with you, attain venerable age. Never silence or chide them, but communicate with them always in tones of deep respect. Be motivated by true compassion, surrender humbly to their wishes, sacrifice your own selfish interests and pray intensely: "Most precious Allah, please shower Your most tender Mercy upon my parents who nurtured and trained me with loving care and patience."

My cherished ones on the Path of Love, Allah Most High knows precisely what intentions abide in your hearts and how selflessly you are committed to goodness. Allah Most Merciful heals with His loving and fragrant forgiveness those who have acted unlovingly but who sincerely rededicate their lives to the Source of Love. My dear human beings who long to be truly human, you must continually offer loving service to all persons as your own extended family, particularly to travelers and to those in need. Never waste any of the resources you have been given by the Source of Life, for those who squander are followers of the cosmic rebel Satan, whose essential rebellion is ingratitude. You must turn aside from people who would consume your gifts fruitlessly without being thankful to Allah Most High, but speak kind and gentle words to them, praying inwardly to the Source of Wisdom and Power for their guidance and protection.

My dear human beings who are awakening to Divine Love, you must be neither reluctant to give nor indiscriminate in giving. If you are only generous to those who feel no gratitude toward the Supreme Source, they will take whatever you have and reproach you for not giving more. Allah alone grants abundance to some and disciplines others with privation, for the Source of Wisdom knows intimately what every being needs for its spiritual evolution. Do not try to take the welfare of the universe into your own hands, but be the selfless and effective instruments of Allah's Own boundless Generosity. The Source of Love and Power radiates directly through His most humble servants.

—Meditation on *Holy Qur'an* 17:22–30

❧

Most Precious Allah

Those wholly in awe of the exaltedness of Allah, who live constantly expecting the Day of Truth, will ascend through the subtle dimensions of Paradise, praising the Source of Beauty ceaselessly: "Most precious Allah, who can deny Your boundless Generosity?" They will discover that these timeless gardens contain all the flowering branches of wisdom, and they will exclaim: "Most precious Allah, who can deny Your boundless Generosity?" They will find two free-flowing springs of Living Water, the second more radiant than the first, and they will cry aloud: "Most precious Allah, who can deny Your boundless Generosity?" They will taste two kinds of every spiritual fruit, the second more subtle than the first, as they pray repeatedly: "Most precious Allah, who can deny Your boundless Generosity?" Reclining on silk carpets of contemplation that are trimmed with the gold brocade of ecstasy, surrounded by the fruits of all spiritual states and stations, they will reflect deeply: "Most precious Allah, who can deny Your boundless Generosity?"

These souls will perceive the Beauty of Allah as luminous maidens whose glances of love express perfect purity and whose being is not touched by the shadow of any limited desire, and they will proclaim: "Most precious Allah, who can deny Your boundless Generosity?" As they discover that the intimate mystery of Divine Beauty is like the warm glow of the ruby and the delicate colors of coral, the constant song of their hearts will be: "Most precious Allah, who can deny Your boundless Generosity?"

My Beloved, the Source of Love, Who is now speaking through you, will announce to these blessed souls: "Can My Response to your beautiful lives of goodness be any less than to

offer you My Own Goodness and My Own Beauty?" Overwhelmed, they will reply simply: "Most precious Allah, who can
deny Your boundless Generosity?"

—Meditation on *Holy Qur'an* 55:46–61

Responsibility

My beloved Muhammad, please instruct those to whom the
Ultimate Source has granted vast earthly wealth to pour forth
generously the abundance they have gratefully received. Teach
those whose provisions are limited to share without hesitation
whatever comes to them from the Source of Life. Allah Most
Wise decrees different forms of responsibility for each soul, yet
never requires any soul to bear a burden which is not already
being borne for it by the Source of Power. As the soul courageously meets each test and discipline, delight, and sweetness
flow into it directly from the Source of Love.

—Meditation on *Holy Qur'an* 65:7

Camphor and Ginger

The Source of Life, Who is now speaking, evolves each human
form from a single drop. This birth and life are, from the very
beginning, testing and teaching for the soul. The Source of Power
designs the human being to hear sensitively and to perceive clearly.
The Source of Love guides humanity to the Direct Path that
returns into the One Source, whether or not any person feels
grateful for this precious guidance. The Source of Wisdom prepares

the sleep of death for those who have lived in negation of Love, so they may be purified by the terrible dreams of Hell in which the Splendor of Allah appears as a blazing fire where they are tightly bound. The lovers of Love awaken instantly from death and recognize the true nature of the Divine Radiance, which they experience as the luminous and ever-flowing spring of plenitude, where devoted servants of Allah Most High fill their silver and crystal cups of prayer with the drink of Divine Love, its delicate flavor as healing and as soothing as camphor.

During their earthly careers, these servants of Love courageously fulfill their sacred vows and meditate constantly on the Last Day that is winging toward them. These humble servants, moved purely by love for the Source of Love, present food and other provisions to the poor, the orphans, the prisoners. To these recipients of Allah's Generosity, My true servants proclaim: "We bring these gifts to you spontaneously, longing only to gaze into the Face of Love. You need never offer us any return, nor need you be grateful to us. We have been inspired to give through our constant contemplation of the universal Mercy of Allah." Through this life of service the Source of Love purifies the lovers of Love, transforming them into beautiful beings, radiant and sweet, who will never need the terrible forms of Divine Purification.

For their patient and dedicated earthly lives, these devoted servants are rewarded with the complete treasure of Love, which they experience as peaceful gardens of Grace and silken garments of Grace. Reclining on thrones of ceaseless contemplation, they are no longer burned by the relentless sun and bitter cold of earthly passion and depression, but abide in refreshing coolness like springtime shade, the fruits of holy wisdom bending branches low around them, as though the very trees of Paradise were bowing humbly before Allah. These lovers of Love share among themselves every level of spiritual experience, drinking together from various mystic vessels—some of silver, some of crystal, and some with the silver of Divine Love and the crystal of Divine Peace combined in harmonious measure.

In the transcendent garden of realization, My lovers are given the drink of illumination, from the primordial fountain whose mystic name is Forever Seeking, and whose sweet flavor burns sharply like ginger. The Attributes of Allah Most High are manifest to My lovers there as eternal youths so beautiful that, when gazed upon, their forms disappear and they become bright pearls, scattered everywhere. Contemplating these luminous pearls, My perfect lovers are lifted to the exalted state of Allah's Own Delight.

Those of My lovers who reach this highest realization are dressed in the silken robes of My constant Presence radiating the Light of Wisdom. These dark green robes of peace are trimmed with the brilliant gold brocade of ecstasy. My truly selfless lovers, bright in countenance, wear the shining bracelets of ceaseless prayer, and their precious Allah offers them directly the most sublime drink of all, the mystic wine of union, placing these Divine Words within their hearts: "Gaze upon all this, which is nothing other than My intense love for you and My complete acceptance of your highest spiritual intentions."

—Meditation on *Holy Qur'an* 76:2–22

Authentic Witness

My beloved Muhammad, please bear this Divine Message in your own being for the very being of humanity: "My eternal human souls, did the Source of Love not find you living as orphans in time, separated from Love, and restore you to communion with Love? Did the Source of Wisdom not find you lost in self-imposed exile, wandering away from the Living Truth, and offer you the clarity of true guidance? Did the Source of Life not find you destitute, struggling to fulfill basic needs through the exercise of your own limited powers, and pour limitless Power and Abundance into your lives?

"Therefore, My cherished human beings who long to become truly human, open your hearts completely to the orphans, and lovingly pour forth your earthly and heavenly wealth to anyone who is in material or spiritual need. This life of compassionate action will be the authentic witness, for all humanity to see, that you have consciously received such bountiful gifts from Allah All-Merciful."

—Meditation on *Holy Qur'an* 93:6–11

True Gratitude

The primary spiritual weakness of human beings is their lack of constant, heartfelt gratitude directed solely toward the Source and Goal of the Universe. The daily existence of humanity testifies clearly to this fundamental thanklessness. People commit vast amounts of energy to acquiring and enjoying the abundant goods of earthly life, without making any real efforts to know and consciously to praise the Source of Life.

At the end of time, those asleep in death will suddenly awaken, and the secrets of every heart and mind will shine forth, illuminated by the Source of Light, Who is so intimately acquainted with all souls. On that infinite Day humanity will recognize its own extreme ingratitude, and will humbly know true gratitude at last.

—Meditation on *Holy Qur'an* 100:6–11

⚘

Compassionate Action

How can one recognize a person who secretly regards the principles of Islam as mere imagination and the Day of Truth as empty myth? This is the person who ignores the needs of orphans, and who is not actively engaged in feeding the hungry with earthly and heavenly nourishment. Those who make a display of piety but have not committed their whole lives to compassionate action are like those who perform daily prayers as habit or as convention, without true awe, humility, and longing. These are the ones who are inwardly turning away from Allah Most High. Since their religion remains mere pretense, the vessel of their being has not been filled with active kindness by the Source of Love.

—Meditation on *Holy Qur'an* 107:1–7

COMMENTARY

Pilgrimage and the Journey of the Soul

The Qur'an encourages Muslims to perform an outer pilgrimage to Mecca at least once in their lives, following various ritual steps that can be seen to emulate the soul's journey through life. Throughout the Qur'an, the metaphor of the journey reminds the listener that, as the soul seeks to return to its primordial state in the heart of Allah, it undergoes struggle, change, and growth and so fulfills its sacred destiny. No one soul's purpose in life is exactly like that of another. Following the lead of the Qur'an, the classical Sufis later formulated various versions of the states and stages of the spiritual journey and saw the ultimate Ka'bah, the center around which the human spirit circled, as the heart itself. As one mystic remarked, we make the whole journey of life simultaneously to Allah, with Allah, and in Allah.

—Ed.

Pilgrimage

The Source of Wisdom first revealed to the noble Abraham the nature of the Holy Ka'bah, the mystic focal point for direct access to Allah Most High within His Creation: "My beloved Abraham, as you construct the sacred cube, the symbolic dwelling of Allah, be sure that no one considers it to be on the same level of reality as the Source of Reality, Who is now speaking. Purify this six-dimensional structure built by human hands with the conscious offering of each step and each breath to the Source of Life. Those who come to circumambulate the Ka'bah of Divine Mystery and those who orient in its direction their prayerful prostrations to Allah Most Sublime, wherever they may be, will therefore be purified from all limited concepts, for their devotion will be to Allah alone and not to His symbolic dwelling. Please teach humanity the powerful practice of pilgrimage to the Ka'bah of Divine Presence as a clear reflection, on this earthly plane, of the soul's heavenly journey to the Source of Love. Traveling to this sacred center by every means, along every path, and from every distance imaginable, pilgrims will approach—humble, barefoot, simply clad—and circle this six-sided crystal, which focuses the Light of Truth. These pilgrims of peace will participate in the mystery of the manifest Presence of Allah and will learn profound spiritual lessons.

"My beloved Abraham, instruct the pilgrims to sacrifice with loving gratitude, while concentrating on the Majestic Name of Allah Most High, some of the flocks that the Source of Life has provided to them for sustenance. This spiritually nourishing food should be prepared not just for themselves but to feed any poor or hungry person they meet. My intimate friend, exhort those who become pilgrims to leave behind from that moment all carelessness, to fulfill their deepest holy vows, and to circumambulate with total purity of attention and intention the manifest abode of the Ultimate Source."

—Meditation on *Holy Qur'an* 22:26–9

The Immense Journey

The Source of Life, Who is now speaking, evolves the human organism from earthly substance, beginning as a minute drop held safely by the vessel of the womb. From that essential drop, the Source of Power develops the structure of cells which gradually becomes living tissue. Then the Power of Allah causes bones to form within that tissue, and finally clothes the organic being with delicate human features.

The immense journey begins as the infant is brought forth from the world of the womb by Allah Most High to become a new creature in a new realm. The profound blessing of each beautiful process of Creation originates directly from the Source of Creation, Allah All-Merciful.

The immense journey reaches culmination when the human being completes its destined span of earthly existence. Plunging through the sleep of death, the soul awakens into the Day of Truth as a new being of light standing in the Direct Presence of Allah Most Sublime.

The Source of Power radiates seven heavenly planes for the soul to ascend gradually, just as the child in the womb develops gradually. With infinite care has the Source of Love designed this mysterious and awesome journey of transformation.

—Meditation on *Holy Qur'an* 23:12–7

ↂ

Open Desert and Dark Sea

The concepts and projects of those who turn away from the Ultimate Source and Goal of the Universe are like illusory appearances in the open desert which wanderers, consumed by thirst, may imagine to be water. When anyone actually attempts to draw life-giving refreshment from such thoughts and actions, there is nothing there. Discovering the complete emptiness of these illusions, the wanderer will finally encounter the Ever-Present Source, Who calls Itself by countless Divine Names and Who pours forth abundantly whatever each person deserves.

Understand the lives of those who turn away from the

Supreme Source to be like dim shadows cast upon the waves of a stormy sea, covered by billows of mist, and above that, by many layers of cloud. This negative mode of existence is a sea so dark that those who sail there can scarcely perceive their own hands. Whoever fails to turn around completely toward the Source of Light lives in ambiguity and deep obscurity.

—Meditation on *Holy Qur'an* 24:39–40

Divine Permission

No suffering or disaster of any kind befalls any being except by the mysterious permission of Allah Most Merciful, to serve as teaching, testing, or chastening for the soul. The minds and hearts of those who can joyfully accept this astonishing truth, and who thereby turn in complete and blessed submission to Allah Most High, will be guided by the Source of Wisdom and comforted by the Source of Love. The Ultimate Source is the Perfect Knower, Who alone can make this awesome proclamation concerning the all-encompassing Divine Permission.

—Meditation on *Holy Qur'an* 64:11

Full Moon

My beloved Muhammad, the Source of Wisdom, Who is now speaking through you, promises souls that they will progress and ascend through realms and levels of spiritual experience as the glowing twilight of human knowledge disappears into richly enveloping blackness, the night of homecoming into Divine Mystery. Then the full moon of Truth will burst forth suddenly from behind the mystic mountain.

—Meditation on *Holy Qur'an* 84:16–9

❧

The Steep Ascent

Has not the Ultimate Source designed the human being as the most sublime instrument? The Source of Power evolves human eyes to perceive and appreciate the Divine Beauty reflected in Creation, human tongue and lips to praise the Source of Creation. The Source of Wisdom empowers each soul to distinguish the way of forgetfulness from the way of constant remembrance of Allah Most High. Yet human beings, bearing these holy gifts, are still reluctant to make the steep ascent of true spiritual practice, which is prayerful contemplation expressed through compassionate action. Who are those who make this ascent, My beloved? They are the merciful ones who free anyone who is enslaved and feed anyone who is hungry, even when they themselves have not enough to eat. These are the lovers who are truly turned toward the Source of Love and who, expressing patience and tenderness at every moment, constantly encourage humanity to remain committed to the holy way of life. My beloved Muhammad, these are your intimate companions.

—Meditation on *Holy Qur'an* 90:8–17

Humanity

My noble Messenger, offer your people the perfect sanctuary, where the human heart becomes the sweet fig tree and the mind the nourishing olive tree, where the soul becomes the sacred mountain Sinai, and the secret essence of the soul becomes the mystical and inviolable city Mecca. The Single Source, Who is now speaking, did indeed create humanity as the most marvelous of all spiritual vessels, although Allah Most High also gives human beings the freedom to negate, which can allow them to degenerate into the most base of all creatures.

To those who, with their very life breath, affirm the Source of Love, and who transform their daily lives entirely into expressions of Love, Allah Most Merciful offers the eternal treasure of His Love. How could any person sensitive to truth fail to experience complete trust and confidence in the Day of Judgment? Is Allah Most High not more compassionate and just than any earthly judge imaginable?

—Meditation on *Holy Qur'an* 95:1–8

The House of Allah

My beloved Muhammad, please remind those to whom the Source of Power has granted sustenance and protection throughout the winters and summers of their lives to offer their very being to the Source of Being, Whose Divine Presence is focused on earth through the mysterious blackness of the Holy Ka'bah, the House of Allah, the secret heart of humanity that is empty of images, concepts, and limits.

—Meditation on *Holy Qur'an* 106:1–4

Struggle with the Small Self: Honesty and Justice

The Qur'an also mentions *jihad*, literally "struggle," as a dimension of living a sacred life. The so-called "Holy War" is not a pillar of Islam, however, and in any offensive sense, is an innovation from after the time of Muhammad. Every battle fought by the young Muslim community during Muhammad's lifetime was defensive. When the early Muslim community finally returned to Mecca, shortly before Muhammad's passing, the Prophet famously said that the time for the lesser, outer struggle was over and the time for the greater, inner struggle (*mujahid*) with one's own self-centered tendencies was to begin.

The Qur'an repeatedly enjoins all Muslims to act with honesty and justice, not only towards other Muslims but towards everyone they meet.

—*Ed.*

The Commitment to Justice

To Allah alone planetary and celestial existence belong as myriad rays belong to the single sun. The Original Source of Light now shining through you, My beloved one, has transmitted an illuminating Book of Revelation to many peoples, through many languages, expressing always the essential message: "Turn with

awe toward the Ever-Present Source alone." Whether or not this
Message of Truth is heeded, the fact remains that the entire spectrum of earthly and heavenly existence emerges from and returns
to Allah alone. Allah is utter Completeness and is alone worthy
of eternal praise.

Allah Most High is the Source of Life streaming constantly
through the lives of earthly and heavenly beings, all of whom He
protects and guides from within by the Power of His Very Presence. If Allah so wished, He could allow humanity to disappear,
and evolve another form of conscious being to express the highest Truth, for Allah alone is the Living Power that manifests His
entire universe in detail, moment by moment. Whoever longs
for fullness and abundance of life should live in conscious surrender to the Source of Life, for Allah alone grants the gifts of
this world and the gifts of Paradise. Allah is the embracing Awareness, Who sees all actions and motivations and Who hears the
most secret prayers.

My cherished lovers who have turned around toward your
own True Source, be utterly committed to justice. Allah Most
High is the Living Truth, and you should always witness to the
truth on every level, even when your personal interests or those
of your family and friends must be sacrificed. Whether rich or
poor, all persons must receive equal justice for Allah Most Merciful is equally present to all. My dear human beings who long
to become truly human, you must never act capriciously or evasively but always in deep accord with the principles of justice
revealed by Allah Most Wise, Who is fully aware of every intention of every being on every plane of Being.

—Meditation on *Holy Qur'an* 4:131–5

Holy Warfare

My cherished human beings who wish to commit yourselves to the struggle of becoming truly human, why are you faint-hearted when faced with the need to sacrifice your individual lives in order to turn completely toward the Source of Life? Are you really content to remain imprisoned within your own limited concepts and selfish concerns? Are you not longing for the Bliss and Peace of Allah, called Paradise, which can only be entered after the death of all anxious turning toward the limited self? Compared with the limitless joy of spiritual awakening, or Paradise, the limited enjoyments that individuals cling to are shallow indeed. My dear human beings, if you fail to participate fully in Holy Warfare against selfishness and negativity, the Greater Warfare carried on invisibly within your own minds and hearts, you must continue to undergo the Divine Chastening that is human suffering. The Ever-Present Source draws innumerable beings into the sacred struggle of purification and homecoming, so this universal spiritual Warfare will continue whether you abstain or oppose. No power can obstruct Allah Most High, Who is the Source of Power.

—Meditation on *Holy Qur'an* 9:38–9

The Call to Justice

My noble Messenger, please remind humanity ceaselessly of the Final Day, when the Supreme Source will call forth from every people a wise and impartial witness to the actions and intentions of that people, both individual and communal. You will be the witness for the vast spiritual nation of Islam. The Ever-Present Source shines this Book of Light through you to clarify the very nature of Creation, to guide the hearts of human beings, to heal with its merciful touch, and to bring joyous illumination to those who consciously receive their lives directly from the Source of Life. Remind your people that the deep human response for which Allah Most Merciful calls is the commitment to justice that transforms daily life into continual acts of kindness and generosity toward all persons, recognizing them as one intimate family. Compassionately warn your people that they are turning away from the Source of Love by performing actions insensitive to the dignity of any being, and that only constant remembrance of the Source of Being can develop true sensitivity. Allah Most High requests humanity to meditate earnestly on His Call to Justice.

There is a primordial covenant between human beings and the Ultimate Source, enacted before the Creation of time or eternity. Allah promises to turn toward the soul and the soul promises to turn toward Allah. No promise, once sworn to, should ever be broken, whether it be the supreme promise to remember Allah Most High or the simple agreements made during daily life. When human beings commit themselves utterly to justice and the constant remembrance of Allah, the Source of Love and Power radiates directly through whatever they do.

—Meditation on *Holy Qur'an* 16:89–91

The Parable of Pride and Submission

There were two neighbors. For one of them the Source of Abundance provided rich grape orchards surrounded by extensive groves of date palms. Between these groves and orchards, through blessings showered from the Source of Life, fertile fields of grain were flowering. The land yielded abundant harvest season after season, for the Source of Power caused an unfailing spring to gush forth there. This is the profound fruitfulness of human life when received as pure Divine Gift. Yet the man whose existence was so blessed by Allah Most High remarked to his neighbor: "Our holdings are similar, but my land yields more wealth because I am more powerful than you." Proud of what he mistook to be the fruits of his own personal power, this person committed injustice against his own soul by allowing spiritual distortion to grow within him, until one day he proclaimed with supreme arrogance: "I am in complete control of my existence. My good fortune can never diminish. Allah will certainly not bring this world to an end during my lifetime and when I die, Paradise will be even more pleasant than my present surroundings."

His neighbor, a soul devoted to the Living Truth, warned the proud man with compassionate and gentle words: "Consider carefully what you are saying, my friend. How can you assume so much? Have you forgotten that the Power of Allah evolved you from a mere drop of earthly substance, gradually shaping your body and mind? Our lives depend solely upon the Source of Life, and we should never turn away from the Source of Power by exalting any power in the universe, including our own. My dear neighbor, when you behold your flourishing orchards, groves, and fields, simply affirm: 'All this abundance comes from the Will of Allah, for there is no power apart from the Source of Power.' Although I have less wealth, Allah Most Merciful has granted me clear understanding, more precious than all your valuable holdings. If you continue to turn toward your own personal power, my friend, the Source of Power could send bolts of lightning during the night and the morning light would reveal only barren ground where green fields once grew. Or one day you could find your gushing spring sunk deep into the earth and your soil turning to dust."

But the one who had allowed severe spiritual distortion to develop within him could not appreciate the wise words of his neighbor, and one dawn he did indeed awake to find his groves and orchards withered, his fields barren, and his wealth dissipated. Clenching his hands in anguish, he cried out: "Why did I equate my own power with the Power of Allah?" The personal power and possessions in which he had taken such pride had totally disintegrated, leaving him helpless in every way.

My cherished human beings, your lives can be protected and elevated only by surrendering them completely to the Source of Life. To submit to Allah Most High is to know and to embrace the truth that there can be only one Supreme Source. To be called along the Path of Submission and to return directly into the Source of Love is the most precious Divine Gift of all.
—Meditation on *Holy Qur'an* 18:32–44

Dishonesty

Any form of outward or inward dishonesty generates severe distortion of heart and mind. Sorry indeed will those persons be who take the full payment given to them, but who return less than honest payment and service to others. Do those human beings who defraud themselves and others in countless ways not realize that they will be awakened on that awesome Day of Days, when every soul stands naked and transparent before the Very Source of Light and Truth?

—Meditation on *Holy Qur'an* 83:1–6

❧

Turning Away

Turning far away from the Source of Love is every person who engages in cruel criticism, or who speaks the slightest untruth about another. Turning even farther away from the Ever-Present Source are those obsessed with selfish accumulation of worldly wealth and authority. They are caught in the basic illusion that riches and power can fulfill the natural longing of the soul for its own True Source.

—Meditation on *Holy Qur'an* 104:1–3

❧

Worldly Authority

Please observe how the Source of Power now speaking deals with arrogant human beings who storm and plunder the earth, mounted on elephants of worldly authority. All the creatures of Allah Most High instinctively direct their energy against these treacherous ones, and the Source of Power dramatically reduces to naught their ambitious plans of conquest. They eventually become like mere fields of straw, whose original fruitfulness has been utterly devoured.

—Meditation on *Holy Qur'an* 105:1–5

The Delirium of Hell

The personal power of the ruthless man will perish at the moment of his death. None of the wealth or influence accumulated in this world will protect him during the final journey of his soul. Their earthly existence of constant selfish grasping will cause such a man and his wife, who indulges with him in the bitter negation of Love, to become lost in the delirium of Hell when they fall asleep in death—he stung with the flames kindled by his own earthly conflicts, she carrying the firewood of consuming ambition, the palm fibre rope of obsession taut around her neck.

—Meditation on *Holy Qur'an* 111:1–5

COMMENTARY
Lovers of Love: A Life of Compassion

Despite what is portrayed in some Western media, and often misunderstood by Muslims themselves, wearing a particular dress or attire is not a "pillar" of Islam. That it has become so important in the last hundred years says more about political and cultural struggles for identity that arose between Europe and the Muslim world than about the original nature of Islam itself, which was intended to embrace all peoples, races, and cultures. Needless to say, the interpretation of the various Islamic practices and what constitutes the absolute essentials of *shariah*, the way of Islam, remains a controversial point amongst Muslims themselves to this day.

The Qur'an repeatedly emphasizes living a life of modesty, gratitude, honesty, justice, compassion, and love. More than any outward signs of piety, it sees these qualities as identifying the real Muslim, the person surrendered to the One Reality. The Sufis found in the Qur'an permission to pass on the inner way it describes through a ritual sometimes called "taking hand," which initiated a spiritual companionship between two people on the path of illumination. Lex Hixon translates the pertinent passage below.

Ultimately, the "Lovers of Love" described by the Qur'an are those who become their own miracles of compassion and peace, whether they come to public attention in the world or not.

—*Ed.*

⚬

Lovers of Love

Regarding spouse and children, gold and silver, fine horses, livestock, and land as expressions of personal power is the way of gratification that glitters with false beauty. But life on Earth lived gracefully as an affirmation of Love, which culminates by returning to the Source of Love, is beautiful indeed. My beloved Muhammad, invite humanity with these words: "Shall I inform you of a truly beautiful way and goal of life?"

Those whose whole being is turned in purity of heart toward the Radiance of Allah Most High will begin to envision Paradise here and will awaken after the sleep of death into gardens of nearness flowing with rivers of peace. Abiding there at the Source of Love, at home in the mystical contentment beyond time, souls share the purest companionship, which delights them far more than passionate love delights those here on Earth.

Allah Most Merciful is intensely aware of His selfless lovers, whom He teaches to pray spontaneously with every breath: "Most precious Allah, we long only to affirm Love. While we exist on earth, please dissolve our denials of Love, so we may experience Your Direct Presence not as the fire of purification but as the radiance of Paradise." These are the lovers of Love who continuously turn from the limited self toward the limitless Source. This constant returning enables them to be profoundly patient, truthful, obedient to the holy way of life, and generous with their wealth and kindness to all beings. Throughout the night and at the dawn prayer these lovers of Allah Most Sublime implore His Forgiveness for any selfish thought or action they have committed knowingly or unknowingly.

My beloved, the Ever-Present Source now speaking through you stands as the primary witness that there is only one Supreme Source, Who calls Itself Allah. This truth of unity is witnessed also by eternal angelic beings, and by human beings who have been awakened to the knowledge of their own True Source and who can therefore remain constant in the way of universal harmony and justice. There is nothing to rely upon other than Allah Most High, Who is limitless Power and perfect Wisdom.

—Meditation on *Holy Qur'an* 3:14–8

∞

Servants of Love

Those who lovingly serve the Source of Love walk gently on this Earth, responding humbly even to foolish or aggressive words with the dignified salutation: "Peace be unto you." These servants of Divine Love often spend the entire night in prayerful prostration and meditation dedicated to the Ever-Present Source. They pray continuously: "Most precious Allah, please deliver all humanity from the Final Chastening, the experience of Your beautiful Radiance as consuming fire, that most terrible station along the way of purification."

These most loyal and devout servants of Love share generously, but never indiscriminately, whatever spiritual and earthy
abundance is granted them by the Source of Love. Their surrendered lives of constant giving are graceful and harmonious. They
never rely upon any power other than the Source of Power, nor
do they transgress the principles of reverence for life revealed
through the noble Prophets by the Source of Life. These lovers
are never promiscuous with their love, for that is turning away
from the Source of Love. When any negation of Love becomes
chronic, it must be purified by Divine Chastening on the Day of
Truth. As for those who repent their negation immediately by
reaffirming the Source of Love, thus aligning their entire lives
with Divine Love, their careless actions of the past will be an-
nulled by Allah Most High, and their being will become
completely filled with goodness. The fundamental Attribute of
Allah is tender Mercy. His Forgiveness is absolute. Whoever re-
pents negative thoughts or actions and demonstrates this by
faithfully following the holy way of life turns around once more
toward the Source of Love and is truly transformed.

The servants of Love are not involved in the least with
human negativity. When they encounter empty talk or derision,
they ignore it with quiet dignity. When they encounter the demonstrations of Love that flow constantly from the Source of Love,
they are awake and sensitive, free from spiritual deafness or blindness. These servants pray joyously: "Most precious Allah, You
have blessed us with spouses and children who are a wonderful
refreshment to our being. May we be pure channels of Love for
all those who wish to turn toward the Source of Love." For their
patient and enduring service of Love, these humble servants will
be exalted to the highest regions of Paradise, deep within Divine Light. They shall be welcomed there by Allah Most High
with the supreme salutation, "Peace be unto you," and they will

experience the sublime goal of the spiritual path, Allah's Own
Perfect Peace.

—Meditation on *Holy Qur'an* 25:63–76

⚬

One Vast Soul

All that is manifested in the heavenly and earthly realms emanates directly from the Ultimate Source. And Allah Most High,
Who needs absolutely nothing, is all that any being ever needs.
Allah alone receives into His Depth the rivers of praise that flow
spontaneously from the minds and hearts of living beings.

Were all the trees on earth to serve as pens and were the
seven seas to become dark blue ink, the Words of Truth that flow
eternally from the Transcendent Qur'an could never be recorded,
for Allah is boundless Power and complete Wisdom.

The physical Creation and spiritual resurrection of humanity is but the career of one vast soul. The entire drama of this
single soul serves only to express the Divine Attributes of the
Hidden Treasure of Love, the One, Who sees all and hears all.

—Meditation on *Holy Qur'an* 31:26–8

⚬

Lovers of Allah

Those who have truly assimilated the demonstrations of Love
that flow from the Source of Love will spontaneously place their
foreheads on the ground, lost in adoration, whenever they are
reminded of Divine Love. These lovers of Allah Most Sublime
will effortlessly chant eloquent hymns of praise, free from any

pride in the power and beauty of their words, liberated from even the slightest awareness of their own limited selves. Immersed constantly in My Love, scorning none of My creatures, these lovers scarcely sleep, so devoted are they to the practice of prayer, invoking Allah Most High throughout the night with ecstatic expectancy and awe. During the day, they tirelessly share with all beings whatever abundance the Source of Life has provided for them. No one can imagine what spiritual sweetness and repose are experienced by these lovers inwardly as My Direct Response to their lives of dedication and generosity.

—Meditation on *Holy Qur'an* 32:15–7

The Loving Embrace of Allah

The Voice of Truth has never called and sent a Prophet to warn any nation without those who live there in the ease of power and authority rejecting His Messenger. To the noble Prophets sent by Allah Most High these pompous leaders always proclaim: "We seriously question the authenticity of your message." These complacent ones always reason the same way: "Since we are so abundantly endowed with wealth and children, why should we be subject to any Divine Warning?"

The Source of Wisdom tests some souls with abundance and others with privation, but most persons are not aware that their condition in the world at every moment is a subtle trial and teaching from Allah Most High.

Those who claim as their own possession the abundance Allah Most Merciful has granted them must learn that affluence and offspring are not signs of nearness to the Ultimate Source. The real sign of blessedness is the constant turning toward the

Source of Love that transforms every thought and action into an expression of Divine Love. The truly blessed ones, whatever their earthly wealth or power, receive inwardly from the Ever-Present Source treasures beyond all conception and imagination. Plunging through the sleep of death, they will awaken instantly and abide on the most exalted levels of awareness in Paradise, deep within the loving embrace of Allah Most High.

—Meditation on *Holy Qur'an* 34:34–7

Parents

The Source of Love wishes to teach humanity the profound importance of loving-kindness toward parents. The mother bears her child with constant self-sacrifice and gives birth with intense labor. The period of childbearing and weaning is thirty months. This demanding physical and spiritual responsibility of the parents continues until the child grows to maturity and reaches the pivotal age of forty years. At that stage in human development, a person realizes at last the full significance of the gift of loving service offered by parents to their children. The mature person then prays intensely: "Most precious Allah, please open my heart and my entire being that I may be truly thankful for the sustaining love that flowed to me through my mother and my father from the Source of Love. May my own life now become pure loving service, an expression of sheer goodness to delight Your Divine Heart. And may my children in turn dedicate themselves entirely to goodness when they reach maturity, recognizing the Divine Love expressed through parental love. Most precious Allah, at last I have truly entered the way of Islam, bowing with reverence and love, side by side with those whose lives are turned completely toward the Source of Love."

These are the spiritually mature human beings. Allah Most Merciful accepts as a holy offering the purest intentions and actions of their lifetimes, dismissing completely their negative deeds and thoughts. These noble servants of Love already abide mystically in Paradise as they live out their dedicated existence on earth. Their radiant mode of being illuminates for all humanity My Promise of Truth, as the devout lives of their parents did before them.

—Meditation on *Holy Qur'an* 46:15–6

Taking Hand

My beloved Muhammad, those blessed companions throughout time who spiritually clasp your right hand with intense love and loyalty are pledging and connecting their lives, through you, directly to the Ultimate Source, Who is now speaking. Allah's Hand of Power is joined mystically with their own right hands. Those who break this sacred oath, this bonding with the Ultimate Source, suffer devastating loss. Those who honor with their very life-breath this holy covenant with Allah Most High will receive the entire treasure of Love directly from the Source of Love.

—Meditation on *Holy Qur'an* 48:10

The Soul's Light

My cherished human beings who long to become truly human, sincerely turn away from your various negations of Love, and let your whole lives affirm Love alone. Your negative deeds and thoughts will then be entirely erased through the mysterious Will of Allah, and you will be awakened fully into Divine Love, which will appear to your spiritual vision as vast gardens and flowing rivers, composed purely of light from the Source of Light. On this Day of Awakening, the Ultimate Source will exalt My beloved Muhammad and those who have witnessed to the truth of his Prophethood. The soul's light of these spiritual companions of My noble Prophet will lead them unerringly as they race in ecstasy deep into the Source of Love. This light from the Source of Light will shine through the right side of their being, indicating profound purity of heart. As they advance, they will be immersed in prayer, calling inwardly: "Most precious Allah, please continue to refine and exalt the light of our souls, forgiving every selfish action or intention of our entire lifetime, for You alone, the Source of Power, have the power to purify us utterly."

—Meditation on *Holy Qur'an* 66:8

THE QUR'ANIC VISION:
WORLDVIEW OF ISLAM

Through His Holy Qur'an, God asks humanity this penetrating question: "Can the knowledge of the blind person be equal to the knowledge of one who sees?" (Sura 6:48–50) Without authentic revelation, human beings remain blind to the full implication of the universe and of their own precious lives. The holy prophets of all nations are the ones who truly see. With minds and senses illuminated by Divine Light, they are free from the various self-centered and self-circumscribed attitudes in which we find ourselves obviously or subtly bound. These illuminated persons alone can plumb the full depth of human experience.

However, God Most High has given every person the gift to see through prophetic eyes. With the help of revealed scriptures and spiritual disciplines, we can awaken directly into the luminous humanity, the fullness of humanity, which the prophets embody. Using the language of these meditations on Qur'anic texts, let us open our eyes and discover what we can see.

THE CREATION

Modern scientific humanity looks upon the universe as essentially a material realm that has come into being from and is governed by material causes. But it is known through prophetic vision as spiritually alive and sensitively governed, the Creation of God Most High that includes both temporal and eternal realms. This Creation is instinctively aware of its own transcendent Source, celebrates its Source, and longs to return to, or consciously unite with, its Source. "Whatever lives in this planetary realm spontaneously celebrates the Source of Life. The birds, simply by spreading their wings for flight, are praising Allah Most High, Who knows intimately the instinctive prayer and praise expressed through the most minute action of every being." (Meditation on *Holy Qur'an* 24:41–5)

The exalted Creator is not simply an impersonal ground of the universe but knows intimately—that is, directly from within each form of consciousness—the prayer and praise that arise not simply from consciously grateful human beings, but from every breath and even every motion of His Creation. "All beings in the universe, whether or not they consciously face their own True Source, are bowing to Allah Most Sublime with their entire being through every thought and action." (13:12–5) The universe revealed by the Qur'an is a Divine Realm, not some disastrous fall away from Divine Existence, nor some merely material domain which exists in outer darkness at the far edge of the Divine Light. "The Supreme Source is the One Light illuminating every heavenly and earthly realm. . . Allah is the One encompassing Awareness." (24:35) The universe is in no fundamental sense negative or tragic. Human beings have the honor and responsibility to engage consciously in its mystic and majestic procession from and return into Godhead. This process is not a total reabsorption into Godhead, but is a continuous home-coming of immense mutual joy and affection. "From Allah alone radiates the great affirmation that is heaven and earth, and to Allah alone, the Source and Goal of Being, is this entire king-dom of Being returning home." (24:41–5)

Again and again God Most High, speaking clearly through His Holy Qur'an, asks humanity to contemplate His Creation—both in its minute detail and in its cosmic scope—as a method for developing spiritual awareness. "Teach them to envision the universe in its original state as an expanse of Light without bor-ders or limits, which the Source of Power gradually shapes into lifebearing worlds. . . .Gazing at this process of Creation with eyes of true understanding, how can anyone fail to see manifest Being as one vast demonstration of Love?" (21:30–3) The Qur'anic revelation never suggests a mechanical or even an or-ganic model of Creation. God never has to struggle with the resistance or seek the cooperation of some inert field of matter or dynamic field of energy. God creates out of nothing, simply by knowing and by effortlessly willing. The resulting Creation, which appears to us in the form of natural processes, expresses the richness and value, the infinite meaningfulness, of the origi-nal Divine Reality. "Whatever is willed by the Source of Being comes spontaneously into Being and bears profound meaning." (24:41–5)

The Creation is a balanced ecology of organic life and spiri-tual meaning. Human beings are divinely appointed as caretakers of God's planetary realm, which is not outside of God but is an intimate dimension of His existence. However, humanity can never claim ownership or control of any aspect of the Divine Creation, which we perceive in limited forms through our lim-ited minds and senses. "The Source of Life evolves innumerable forms of organic life, each in precise balance with the others . . .

human beings do not own or control these natural treasures . . .
all manifest Being belongs solely to the Source and Goal of Being." (15:16–25)

The purpose of the Creation is radically spiritual. The temporal career of the eternal soul is not some lesser phenomenon
in the universal drama of manifestation. The education of the
soul is the central reason for the existence of the universe. "His
entire Creation exists simply as testing and teaching for the soul."
(11:7–11) Therefore the soul—that is to say, the ray of eternal
awareness focused through suitably advanced life-forms on life-
bearing planets throughout the universe—is at the very center
of the drama of God's Creation. The soul is not an insignificant
spark of life in an unknown and unknowing expanse of galaxies,
as imagined by the modern scientific world view. By truly knowing ourselves, we know directly the essence and purpose of the
whole Creation. We are not groping in darkness.

This supremely advanced and supremely humane spiritual
knowledge, far beyond the possible range of science or even philosophy, cannot be attained without the process of Divine
Revelation. Revealed truth, however, is not imposed upon the
human being from the outside but is integral to the very life of
the soul and is therefore immediately recognizable to the depths
of human awareness. Revelation is welcomed by the soul and is
never considered strange or foreign by the mature, or fully awakened, consciousness of the human being, who is, as the Holy
Qur'an reveals, the very crown of God's Creation. This level of
human dignity and calm certainty cannot be imagined or attained without revelation.

Prophetic vision does not perceive Creation as flat—we
smile at medieval European cartographers who pictured the earth
as flat—but as a hierarchical structure of planes or spheres. The
terminology of above and below is used, but not in a spatial

sense. Above the planetary plane, which includes all life-bearing planets, there extend seven subtle planes of Being, which are richly populated by conscious beings, expressing entirely distinct orders of reality. Above the subtle planes exists the most sublime created realm, which in the Qur'anic vision contains both eternity, the abode of angels, and Paradise, the abode of souls. "The body in Paradise will emanate from the same Source of Light that has projected this earthly body, and that consciously radiates all the vast realms and levels of Creation." (36:77–83) Above Paradise subsists the Garden of Essence to which the mystic lovers and knowers aspire, which is not Creation, neither time nor eternity, but God Himself.

There exists, however, no hierarchy of Divine Presence, because God's Creation is not in any way alienated or distant from its exalted Creator. "During six primal and measureless Days of Power, the Supreme Source radiated the luminous structure of the planetary realm and the seven heavenly realms as tangible and intangible planes of Being. The Source of Being is mystically established upon this vast Throne of Manifestation. The full Divine Presence can therefore be subtly experienced throughout Creation." (7:54–6)

The Qur'anic vision of Creation should not be thought of as abstract or metaphysical. It remains direct and existential, intimately related to our daily experience. "Turn ceaselessly toward Allah Most High, whose Power presents you this green planet as resting place and this brilliant tent of stars as inspiration, Whose Mercy descends as sweet rain to create the earthly fruits you need for sustenance." (2:21–5) Nonetheless, we should not read the Holy Qur'an as some primitive perception of the world which equates, for instance, heavenly realms with the starry night-time sky. "Cosmic space is but the reflection of the lowest and least subtle of the seven heavens and is a reservoir of energy for the preservation of the earthly plane of Being." (41:9–12)

The hierarchical structure of Being exists, not out of some impersonal metaphysical necessity, but precisely for the spiritual elevation of the soul, a process of great delicacy that the Holy Qur'an likens to the development of the fetus in the womb. The higher levels of Being, as well as the planetary plane of existence, are no less than the perfect expression of the infinite Divine Mercy. "So the Source of Power created seven progressively more subtle planes of existence and consciousness, revealing on each plane a new level of love and knowledge for the souls who will return along this path of mystical ascension into the Source of Peace." (41:9–12)

The mystics of Islam find in these Qur'anic texts the confirmation of their own direct inner experience of seven levels of awareness, each one more refined and more extensive, which culminate in the ultimate experience of mystical union. This spiritual culmination, expressed by Sufi poets and described figuratively by God Most High in His Holy Qur'an, remains essentially beyond conception or description, as God Himself does, because this supreme illumination simply is God.

Those truly mature human beings in every culture who actually encounter the universe in this way—not just reading a metaphysical map or following with blind faith, but as a direct vision through prophetic eyes—are described by this meditation on the revealed words of the Qur'an: "Those whose whole being is oriented toward the Source of Being do not perceive the slightest imperfection or injustice in the boundless kingdom of the All-Merciful One." (67:1–4) What humanity, when using its own circumscribed concepts, falsely perceives as a chaotic field of physical energy, as a world of chance and conflict, is truly perceived in the light of revelation as a perfect kingdom. Prophetic consciousness would regard the modern scientific world view not primarily as an advance in knowledge, but as a regression in the sensitivity and depth of knowledge. This regression is not, however, just a characteristic of the contemporary age. The prophets have encountered and opposed similar constructs of human convention in their various native cultures throughout the ages.

The antidote for this conventional thinking, this narrow or selective perception, is not to turn away from the visible universe into speculative metaphysics or into the autostimulation of visionary experiences. The Qur'anic way is to contemplate the created universe anew, with expanded vision. "Perceiving this wondrous Creation of the material body, how can the intelligence of humanity doubt that the Source of Power can recreate human beings after death on immaterial planes of existence." (75:34–40)

An essential aspect of this revealed vision of the universe is the vivid understanding that physical or temporal Creation is not to exist endlessly, any more than it has existed without beginning. When the education and ascension of the souls have been completed according to the impenetrable wisdom and compassion of God, the entire planetary realm and the subtle spheres will be returned into the supreme realm of Paradise. Creation will not disappear, for Paradise is the consummate Divine Creation, but the dramatic play of separation between God and His Creation will come to an end. The contemplation of the end of time, which awakens and intensifies the depths of human awareness, is one of the basic spiritual practices in which God instructs humanity through the revealed verses of the Holy Qur'an. "When time suddenly disappears, in the eternal moment of illumination, the brightness of the heavenly orbs will be extinguished by sheer Divine Splendor and the universe will be split open and dissolved into transparent light. This full revelation of the Source of Light will blow away like mere motes of dust the primordial mountains, the cosmic structures upon which this earthly plane rests so securely." (77:8–15)

This passage is the figurative description of the personal experience at the time of physical death. It also describes the return of all manifest Being into the Source of Being at the end of time, when the process of Divine Creation is fully ripe and reaches its spiritual culmination. No structure of life, no truly living value, personal or universal, is lost during the supreme transition from limited life into Divine Life.

This inspiring contemplation of the created universe in the light of revelation ultimately leads to the contemplation of our own humanity as the crown of Creation, not out of self-congratulation or wish fulfillment but as a genuine opening into awe, wonder, and true worship.

The path of prophetic knowledge is ecstatic in the etymological sense of standing outside the limited self, outside the personal and cultural frontiers whose existence we have proclaimed, innocently or arrogantly, limits which are suffocating to the limitless nature of the eternal soul. With prophetic eyes open, we can consciously enter the beautiful kingdom of Divine Creation for the first time, dancing joyously as the man blind from birth whom the Messiah Jesus healed.

ALLAH MOST HIGH

In Qur'anic tradition, there are ninety-nine principal Divine Names that refer to the single Source of the universe. These are not tentative or speculative human terms for God, but are the beautiful Divine Names themselves, which were revealed by God through His Arabic Qur'an and which attest to the mysterious diversity of attributes within the one Essence. The Arabic form and sound of these names bear the sacramental power of Divine Presence—healing, protecting, and illuminating the person who invokes them. But names of God have been revealed through other prophetic dispensations that are equally to be respected.

Through these mystical names, our conscious being comes into direct contact with the essential energy of the One. This one Reality is not the subject of philosophy but is the Living One who revealed itself to the Prophet Moses from the flames of the burning bush: "The highest Truth is that I alone am." (20:9–39) So when we speak with humility and awe of Allah Most High, we are not referring to some deity, abiding in some heaven, circumscribed by some theology. We are invoking the only I Am, the only Consciousness, who composes whatever exists, and who is infinitely more comprehensive even than existence itself. We therefore cannot hold any theological or philosophical concepts about Allah, much less can we engage in any poetic descriptions of God or limit Him in any way, such as confining Him to one particular revelation.

However, God takes the initiative to reveal Himself to humanity—adequately and fully—through the prophets and the precious books of revelation, which He has transmitted throughout the history of humanity. In fact, the process of revelation is constant and extends far beyond the messages borne by the prophets, for Creation itself is known as the cosmic Qur'an. The human mind cannot confine, systematize, or claim as its own any dimension of this awesome revelation, which is all-inclusive and all-transcending.

When we sincerely invoke any one of the Divine Names of God Most High through the guidance of His prophetic tradition, we enter into an unspeakably direct relationship, an existential union, with the only Reality. "Those who invoke Allah Most Merciful with intense prayer feel immediately the unmistakable Presence of the Living Truth, whereas those who worship various elemental forces or etheric beings do not experience the same flood of encompassing Holy Presence." (13:12–5) The mystical names of God release a flood of spiritual experience, the intense awareness of holy presence, which has been granted to humanity through all revealed traditions. The Divine Names are not words in a dictionary, nor are they separate from the One who is named. There can be no distance between us and the one Reality because apart from the one Reality, nothing exists. This nearness to God, which is, in Qur'anic terms, nearer than nearness, is an expression of the Divine Mercy. "No being can actually move the slightest distance from the Ever-Present Source of Being. The utterly merciful Will of Allah is beyond any comprehension." (14:24–7)

The longing of the mystical lover or the thirst of the mystical knower for the Essence of God finds its Qur'anic base and confirmation in the account of the Prophet Abraham's experience of enlightenment. "His adoration of Divine Attributes disappeared entirely, and he awakened mystically into the Divine Essence alone." (6:74–83)

This supreme realization does not imply, however, that the Mercy, Justice, Majesty, and Beauty of God Most High disappear, or that His Creation disappears. After undergoing this experience of mystic union, the Prophet Abraham returns to his people and takes up the burden of his prophetic role. Awakening into Essence means to realize completely—not through our own limited efforts but as the supremely gracious gift of the All-Merciful One—that God Most High alone exists. No imagined gap remains between His Essence and His blessed expression of that Essence. The illusion of duality, or separation, is all that disappears, leaving the full spectrum of the Creation shining, in Qur'anic terms, as light within Light. Now the conscious

education of our souls can truly begin. "The Single Source behind all beings and events projects this vast drama of life and
death as an education for souls, who learn to express the Beautiful Attributes of Allah through contemplation and action within
the realm of temporality." (67:1–4)

This exalted level of mystic experience, the conscious union
with Essence, is not confined to the Prophet Abraham or to a
few rare souls in the contemplative Orders of the great religious
traditions. Direct and intimate friendship with the Divine Essence is the characteristic of all authentic prophecy and is shared
to some degree by every devout soul who receives the permission
of God to see through the eyes of the holy prophets. God Most
High does not reveal Himself partially but fully, for He is fullness itself, which can never be divided in any way. The Holy
Qur'an counsels not just the prophets, but every human being
without exception, to have recourse directly to the ultimate Reality, without intermediary or hierarchy, without hesitation or
self-depreciation of any kind. "Never resort to magic or cosmic
forces you instinctively know to be secondary, but rely for spiritual strength on the Original Source alone." (2:21–5) Every soul
under the care of the Qur'anic revelation consciously enters the
Divine Essence, Allah Most High, with the powerful words revealed precisely for that purpose by the Essence itself: "I take
refuge in Allah alone, the Supreme Guide of humanity. I take
refuge in Allah alone, the mysterious King of humanity. I take
refuge in Allah alone, the True Source of humanity." (114:1–6)

THE HOLY QUR'AN

The voice of God, speaking through the heart, mind, and
lips of the Prophet Muhammad, clarifies the various levels of

revelation. The cosmic Qur'an is the Creation itself, full of the highest teachings of wisdom.

Every creature that flows as Water of Life from the Source of Life is a parable, spoken by the Cosmic Qur'an that teaches humanity to gaze with eyes of wisdom upon all My Creations. (24:41–5)

The transcendent Qur'an, by contrast, is the very Awareness of God.

There is not even a single grain of sand in the obscure depths of the earth, nor any plant, blooming or withering, that is not recorded in the Transcendent Qur'an, which is the perfectly clear Awareness of Allah. My cherished human beings, this encompassing Divine Awareness receives you into sleep every night and knows intimately what you experience each day. (6:59–62)

All has been recorded from eternity in the boundless Book of Reality, the encompassing Awareness of Allah Most High. (22:67–70)

Every action ever performed by human beings until the end of time, including each thought, significant or fleeting, is already inscribed in the Transcendent Qur'an, the encompassing Awareness of Allah. (54:41–55)

The Arabic Qur'an, which is the historical book we can reverently hold in our hands, is a perfect reflection in temporal human experience of the transcendent Qur'an. Similarly, the Qur'an of the Creation itself is a perfect reflection, on the cosmic scale, of the Qur'an of God's own all-encompassing Awareness. The historical Arabic Qur'an participates fully in the splendor and power of both the cosmic Qur'an and the transcendent Qur'an. The Arabic Qur'an is not essentially a work of human production, but a door opened by God between the dimensions of His one Reality so that humanity may enter the treasure house of His beautiful Divine Names. As such, the

Qur'an is to be regarded with intense awe and reverence, even in its handwritten or printed form, which is merely a symbol for the living Qur'an that consists of the resonance and meaning of these 6,666 verses, held in the memory and chanted with moving power by generation after generation.

The very shapes and sounds of the Arabic letters of the Qur'an are considered to be a mode of access to the spiritual realm of the living Qur'an, to its radiance and resonance and to its union of heart-awakening sound with eternal meaning. "The Ever Present Source thus reveals Eternal Meaning through the medium of time as the resonant chanting of the Arabic Qur'an so that humanity can awaken and truly understand." (12:1–6) The Prophet Muhammad inwardly heard the Arabic verses of the Qur'an. He did not simply encounter the Divine Meaning and compose his own words to express it. Therefore, no translation of the Arabic Qur'an into any language can be the Holy Qur'an, but is simply a human interpretation, which may be inspired but does not exist on the sublime level of revelation.

Nor is the Qur'an, strictly speaking, composed in an ancient form of Arabic. The particular configuration of Arabic which is the Qur'an is a revelation which participates in the infinite meaningfulness and mercy of God, and which can be truly understood and assimilated only with the Divine Permission. Therefore, knowing Arabic from childhood or studying Arabic as a scholar is not what gives one spiritual access to the Holy Qur'an. One is attuned to the Qur'an by receiving it with purity of heart, in the same manner that the prophets received revelation.

Nor is the Holy Qur'an regarded as a particular revelation alone, but as the reservoir of and safeguard for all the revelations sent to the previous prophets of God.

The Holy Qur'an indicates the existence of two main levels of interpretation. Both these levels, or spheres of meaning, are

equally true and complement each other. The full communication of the Divine Meaning is made possible only by Divine
Words which, though clothed in historical Arabic, retain their
infinitely powerful nature and transform human language into a
stream of power and truth. "Words of Truth that have the power
to express the Truth are like flourishing trees whose roots, or
direct meanings, are established deep in the earth of the heart,
and whose branches, or subtle meanings, reach high into the sky
of mystical knowledge." (14:24–7) Both direct meanings and
subtle meanings, and their unique modes of sensitive interpretation, must be employed by those who have been lifted into
intimate spiritual friendship with the Holy Qur'an.

Qur'anic interpretation is not simply a method of scholarship that can be taught in a neutral academic manner. True
understanding of the Qur'an is a gift from God, received through
a life of prayer, through the prayerful study of the writings of the
mature sages of Islamic tradition, and through direct contact
with living persons who embody the beauty and wisdom of the
Qur'anic vision. What results from a subjective or narrow reading of the Qur'an is often a serious imbalance of understanding:
such as the merciless fanaticism of some persons within the Islamic community or the rejection of the Qur'an by some persons
outside this ancient community of faith. "My beloved, the Source
of Wisdom sends these living parables through you to illumine
humanity, but no one can understand them profoundly who has
not received the Divine Gift of mystical interpretation" (29:41–4)
Allah warns again and again that His Holy Qur'an is not a simple
book, to be interpreted literally in the light of limited concepts
and attitudes, either personal or cultural. Though appearing in
written or printed form, the Qur'an is like the burning bush
that Moses faced with awe in the valley of revelation. "This
Revelation is a mysteriously veiled Book of Light, descending

directly from the Source of Light, containing Words of Truth whose secret meanings cannot be touched except with minds and hearts completely purified by Allah Most High." (56:63–80)

God reminds humanity that His Holy Qur'an is not a book of inspired poetry that is only capable of hinting at the Divine Meaning, nor is the immense spiritual attraction of the Qur'an, particularly when chanted, a display of any kind of magical or psychic power. (69:38–51) Allah makes it clear that His Holy Qur'an could never have emanated from any self-appointed powers on the subtle planes of existence, who are either totally confused themselves or who are consciously attempting to draw human beings into the wake of their own spiritual ambition. (81:22–9)

God Most High teaches His Prophet Muhammad to speak in a truly humble and even ordinary manner, quite in contrast to the pretensions, flamboyant actions, and promises of both the charlatans and the honestly misguided religious figures who appear in all cultural contexts. Listen to the quiet balance and tenderness of the mode of speaking dictated to the heart of His Prophet Muhammad by God Most High.

My friends, please do not feel that I am a stranger, for I am an ordinary human being, no different than yourselves. I have humbly received anew the ancient Revelation that all manifest Being emerges from and returns to the Single Source and Goal of Being, Who refers to Itself as Allah and by countless of other Most Beautiful Divine Names. (41:2–8)

THE DRAMA OF REVELATION

The Holy Qur'an never purports to add to, or to subtract from, the essential core of prophetic teachings that belong to all humanity. To respect and accept the Qur'an means to affirm as well all of God's revelations throughout history, which share precisely the same essence. The various Divine Revelations, which have historically developed into the revealed traditions as we know them today, are unique and self-authenticating holy ways of life, not just various sets of doctrines, Although history presents a picture of great religious diversity, God assures humanity in His Holy Qur'an that such diversity should not be regarded as the deviation of one tradition or another from the truth, but as a Divine Mystery that will be explained and illuminated by God Himself in a context of consciousness that transcends history. "The Ever-Present Source has revealed a uniquely authentic holy way to each and every nation, true spiritual disciplines that should be performed with care and constancy . . . . On the Mystic Day when you awaken from the sleep of finite existence, Allah Most Wise will explain clearly to you the diversity that now appears to divide His various Revelations." (22:67–70)

This aspect of the Qur'anic vision, the harmony of religions, represents much more than human generosity, tolerance, and ecumenical spirit. Only God can offer such absolute assurance concerning the unbroken and unbreakable unity of all revealed traditions. This religious unity is not a mere wish, nor an intellectual speculation, nor even a high moral ideal that may or may not be capable of fulfillment. The essential teaching transmitted through all the prophets is stated clearly by God again and again in the Qur'an as revealed truth. It is surprising and direct, full of healing and illuminating power to transform our basic way of experiencing the world. The instinctive feeling of separation between members of different religious or cultural bodies can be dissolved only through contemplating revealed truth and not through the rational and diplomatic processes that allow our self-centered, divisive motivations to continue functioning. "Throughout the course of history the Source of Wisdom has sent Holy Messengers to bear only one essential Message: 'There are no conscious beings separate from the infinite I Am that I am. Therefore surrender your very being to the Source and Goal of Being.'" (21:19–25)

The coherence and inclusiveness of this single message at the center of the drama of revelation is self-evident, not just because it has been stated so clearly by the Holy Qur'an but because it really has been the essential point of all revelations throughout history. This message is self-evident because our consciousness is created to be harmonious with the truth that there is no fundamental separation within the one Reality.

Revelation does not consist only of general principles but is characterized by rich particularity and uniqueness. None of the historical situations that have become vehicles for Divine Revelation are ever to be dismissed in favor of a general theory of revelation. And no previous revelation is meant to be replaced by more recent revelation. The fact of radical religious diversity does create tensions between historical traditions, although according to the Qur'anic vision these feelings of tension or foreignness between the peoples of revelation are to be discarded and God's own explanation is to be humbly awaited. Nonetheless, once the Truth reveals Itself through a unique, unrepeatable historical figure, that person remains a bearer of supreme blessing to humanity for all future ages. Thus the voice of Truth assures the Virgin Mary in the Holy Qur'an:

From before eternity, Allah Most Merciful has ordained this spontaneous childbirth as a unique demonstration of His Love and Compassion for human beings to contemplate throughout history. (19:16–36)

The stature of a Holy Prophet is extremely exalted. Islamic tradition recognizes souls to be eternal by nature, which is to say that God created even from before eternity all the souls who would ever descend into the spatial and temporal realm of history. Among these radiant human souls—each one of whom received as its eternal life the very breath of God, and each one of whom is irreplaceable—the souls of the prophets appear as suns among candle flames, so transparent are they to the boundless Divine Light. As we contemplate the life and teaching of any of the exalted prophets of God, the sense of awe, the sense of gazing at a magnificent rising sun, should pervade our awareness. This overwhelming intuition of prophetic magnificence, which is ultimately the magnificence of truly awakened humanity, is an essential aspect of the Qur'anic vision. "The Source of Wisdom placed from before eternity this penetrating spiritual understanding in the soul of My beloved Abraham so he would be a leader for those who turn with perfect clarity toward Allah alone." (6:74–83) The fact that Jews, Christians, and Muslims have all emerged from the lineage of the Prophet Abraham gives some indication of the measureless stature of this prophetic soul.

In the drama of revelation, however, the life of a Holy Prophet, no matter how glorified his soul, is never without terrible struggle and suffering, is never a fantasy of worldly power and adulation. As God consoles His Prophet Muhammad: "The Holy Messengers before you were also branded as imposters. With patient and unwavering hearts they accepted this calumny, deeply saddened, until the very Source of Love, Who manifests through you, flooded them with Peace and Power." (6:33–4)

Far from being in some fundamental, atavistic competition with one another, the various prophetic revelations confirm, expand upon, and safeguard each other. Once again, this deep perception of harmony is based on revealed truth. It is not just a rational or empirical theory put forward by well-meaning scholars or reformers. As revelation, this universal harmony of religions must be deeply contemplated and prayerfully assimilated rather than debated in the intellectual or political dimensions of our surface awareness. "Through the Prophet Jesus, the Source of Wisdom transmitted the Radiant Gospel, full of the same light of Truth that streams through the Living Torah . . . the Eternal Source now reveals through you, My beloved Muhammad, this sublime Book of Truth, which confirms and safeguards the essential teaching of the Torah, the Gospel, and all the other authentic scriptures that existed before them." (5:49–52) We may wonder why God permits religious diversity and even outright doctrinal contradiction to develop around the essential message of conscious participation in the oneness of Reality. This is similar to another root question: Why did God generate such a diversity of created beings, even in deadly conflict, within the perfect peace of the Divine Unity? The answer is the same: for the spiritual education and strengthening of souls. "The Source of Power could have united all peoples into a single nation, but Allah Most Merciful has chosen to manifest His Truth through various holy traditions as teaching and testing for human beings. If each spiritual nation practices faithfully the path revealed through its own Prophets, then all humanity will return together to the Source of Love." (5:49–52)

This Qur'anic vision of the unity of revelation can bring immeasurable joy and fruitfulness to human life on earth. This internal harmony of all revealed paths to God—this harmony of all existence, for the Creation itself is also revelation—is the natural environment of the soul, not some possible or impossible vision of the future. All the prophets and the scriptures have generated this profound sense of ultimate harmony, without which the human being cannot breathe spiritually and becomes suffocated in the surface conflicts of personal and collective interests, including conflicts of religion. This fresh air of revelation has always existed as the breathable spiritual atmosphere of humanity. "So many of these luminous Messengers have emerged from the human family that there can be no impression that Allah Most Merciful has not spoken repeatedly to all nations." (4:163–6) Through the Holy Qur'an, the voice of Truth clearly and unambiguously invites humanity to global harmony. The Prophet Muhammad was empowered by God to issue a very profound call for universal reconciliation. This call does not represent simply his own broad-mindedness or sense of peaceful diplomacy, which were definitely part of the Prophet's personal way of being, but represents the Divine Initiative revealed through him. These words of truth are spoken to all peoples through the person of the Prophet Muhammad. "I affirm the truth of every Revelation which has come down as a Holy Book from the Source of Truth, and I am instructed by this very Source to be impartial among the Peoples of Revelation. The Ever-Present Source, Who calls Itself by countless Divine Names, is the Source of our spiritual nation and your spiritual nations. We have our integral practice of the holy way of life as you have yours. There need be no fundamental disagreement among us. Allah Most High will draw us together as we return home to the Source of Love." (42:13–8)

The integral nature of each revealed tradition is stressed because human beings need rich, historical soil in which to be rooted. Souls cannot live and grow in strength by floating in an abstract space of general principles. That would be philosophy, not revelation. God wishes to protect the balanced ecology of each living environment of His Revelation. "Thus Jewish and Christian traditions should be accepted reverently in the light of the Glorious Qur'an . . . . But you should not accept, My beloved, any teachings or practices of these earlier traditions which have sprung from limited human conceptions or which contradict the dear principles of truth revealed through the Living Qur'an." (5:49–52) This Divine Warning is not meant to generate an attitude of divisiveness, but simply to sharpen our realistic recognition that the historical process can produce subtle or obvious distortions in any precious body of revelation, which nevertheless remains essentially authentic, pure at its core, and worthy of our reverent acceptance. The decision about which aspects of a given tradition have become distorted is complicated by the chaotic surface of cultural differences as well as by deep problems of communication. To follow this Divine Instruction is not aggressively to criticize other great traditions, but to exist humbly in awe of the Divine Unity while remaining fully integrated with the continuous initiatory transmission of the particular body of revelation in which one actually lives and breathes.

However, the soul is never to be essentially identified with one historical strand of revelation as opposed to another, for we have seen that revelation is one, just as God is one. The Holy Qur'an allows us a precious vision of the one revelation, the religion beyond religions, which nonetheless constitutes the living core of each religion, the religion that is not imposed upon humanity, but that is the very nature of humanity as created by God. "All nations are given precisely the same spiritual instruction from the Source of Wisdom. The Voice of Truth calls human beings to turn around completely toward their own True Source, to plunge wholeheartedly into prayer each day, and to offer constant tenderness and assistance to those in any kind of need. This is the one Religion of Truth, natural to the human soul, which transcends all religious factions with its perfect clarity and directness." (98:1–5)

THE LIFE OF COMPASSION AND LOVE

To conclude this brief exploration of the worldview of Islam, we should observe the actual mode of life enjoyed by persons who see Creation through prophetic eyes. They are primarily persons of peace—the peace that springs from intimately knowing the Divine Unity as mercifully all-inclusive. "When they encounter empty talk or derision, they ignore it with quiet dignity . . . responding humbly even to foolish or aggressive words with the dignified salutation: Peace be unto you." (25:63–76) These persons of love never experience themselves as isolated individuals who must defend any personal, cultural, or religious self-interest. They sense coursing through their limbs and organs at every moment only the one Divine Action. "Those whose entire lives intimately face the Source of Life never grow weary of being channels for Divine Power and are never too proud to serve as humble instruments of Divine Mercy, even in the smallest details of daily life." (21:19–25)

The only real motivation for leading this peaceful, harmonious, and helpful way of life, this life of player revealed to humanity through all the prophets, is to encounter God intimately and completely. "Please encourage those who aspire to Islam to be gentle and selfless, to turn wholeheartedly toward the Source of Being, and to call out to Allah Most Merciful every morning and evening, longing only to gaze directly into the Face of Love." (18:27–31) In the disappearance of all sense of separation, which is the life of true prayer, the human being becomes a conscious expression of the very Divine Love that is adored as the all-encompassing, all-constituting Reality. The fruit of this mystical union is the most sensitive and beautiful ethical life, which is not the response to an ethical imperative but the spontaneous expression of spiritual awakening, the constant affirmation of the one Reality with every thought and every breath. Qur'anic revelation is not a conventional, abstract piety that worships an isolated Supreme Being, but the loving affirmation of all lives within the one Divine Life. "The deep human response for which Allah Most Merciful calls is the commitment to justice that transforms daily life into continual acts of kindness and generosity toward all persons, regarding them as one intimate family . . . . Compassionately warn your people that they are turning away from the Source of Love by performing actions insensitive to the dignity of any being, and that only constant remembrance of the Source of Being can develop true sensitivity." (16:89–91)

The persons whose eyes of wisdom have been opened by the light of revelation to see God constantly are moved to share with others whatever abundance they have received from the Source of Creation. These mature persons never assume any particular outcome of a situation because they accept whatever happens as a deepening of their faith and understanding, and hence they are never aggressive in any sense. "These are My authentic lovers and friends, whose very lives are lived as praise and prayer, whose every act is compassionately to share whatever earthly or heavenly abundance the Ultimate Source has provided for them . . . who regard all events without exception as generous gifts and teachings from the Source of Wisdom." (8:2–4) This transformed mode of living is truly human, not superhuman. It provides the basis for the moral laws of culture, although not itself motivated by questions of legality or morality but, rather, by the instinctive truthfulness of the entire being of the person who experiences God as supremely close to all lives. "Allah Most High is the Living Truth, and you should always witness to the truth on every level, even when your personal interests or those of your family and friends must be sacrificed. Whether rich or poor, all persons must receive equal justice, for Allah most merciful is equally present to all." (4:131–5)

This mode of experiencing, or directly living, the Divine Love on earth is not primarily ethical or rational, but mystical. From this supremely loving perspective, which is really the perspective of Paradise, the world appears in an astonishing light, far beyond any utopian vision, for utopias are mere human speculation, not revealed truth. "The man or woman who lives life completely turned toward the Source of Love, affirming Love with every breath, will encounter Paradise everywhere and will begin to understand the justice rendered to all beings by Allah Most High, justice so perfect that no soul is wronged by even so much as the point of a date stone." (4:116–125) The life of constant, devoted service to fellow beings, which is the way of life revealed universally through all the prophets, is not a program of social action but a form of meditation on the Divine Love. This holy way of life consists of spontaneous acts of generosity that are inspired by a constant inner awareness of the Divine Generosity. The verses of the Holy Qur'an are the Words of God, not the secular philosophy of social reform. Yet truly dedicated service to society can and must be fruitfully undertaken with prophetic vision. "These humble servants, moved purely by love for the Source of Love, present food and other provisions to the poor, the orphans, the prisoners. 'We bring these gifts to you spontaneously, longing only to gaze into the Face of Love. You need never offer us any return, nor need you be grateful to us. We have been inspired to give through our constant contemplation of the universal Mercy of Allah.'" (76:2–22)

There is a mystical revolution of consciousness contained in this act of supreme worship, this selfless giving of our whole being to God through the loving service of fellow human beings. The poor, orphans, and prisoners—and most human beings exist under these abject conditions, either in a literal or a figurative sense—are indeed the secret bearers of the Divine Essence. By offering humanity love, the truly awakened servants of God are worshipping the Source of Love and gazing intimately into the Face of Love. Humanity's spiritual recognition of its own oneness with Divine Reality is the goal of the prophetic way. "This mission is the progressive awakening of humanity to its essential perfection initiated through the transcendental Adam, before whom even the angels bowed with their whole being . . . the secret essence of the human soul is the encompassing Awareness and complete Wisdom of Allah." (12:1–6)

The Qur'anic description of true mystics, persons who have authentically experienced union with God, is expressed in terms of becoming channels of the Divine Mercy. Unhesitating generosity is the function of spiritual maturity. Every human soul is capable of growing into such maturity. The prophets are not presenting a mystical doctrine open to only a handful of specially motivated or specially qualified individuals. This call to compassion and union is the universal invitation of God, resounding clearly through all the revered prophets of God, and entirely transcending both the external forms of religion and the doctrinal disputes among religions. "Those who make a display of piety but have not committed their whole lives to compassionate action are like those who perform daily prayers as habit or as convention, without true awe, humility, and longing. Since their religion remains mere pretence, the vessel of their being has not been filled with active kindness by the Source of Love." (107:1–7)

This life of total compassion is not a grim responsibility difficult to bear, nor is it a proud sense of duty that makes a person feel immensely important to society. This life of the Divine Love on earth, which is the perfect knowledge of unity, is

primarily an expression of true spiritual joy, arising spontaneously from affirming God with every cell of our body, with every
strand of our awareness. Spiritual joy is not a secret teaching,
but the experience of Divine Love transmitted through the authentic prophets. The Holy Qur'an reveals the ultimate and
perhaps the only question that God puts to the soul. "My dear
humanity, at the dawning of the eternal Day, souls will be asked
whether they have experienced only self-centered pleasure or
whether they know the nature of true spiritual joy. Consider
deeply what your response will be." (102:1–8)

Appendix Two

MEDITATIONS ON THE HOLY QUR'AN
IN THEIR TRADITIONAL ORDER

NOTES

1. For more information on Lex Hixon's life and work, see www.lexhixon.org and www.mightycompanions.org/lexhixon/

2. Schimmel, Annemarie. *Islam: An Introduction* (Albany: State University of New York Press, 1992), p. 48.

3. Translated and quoted in Schimmel, Annemarie. *Deciphering the Signs of God: A Phenomenological Approach to Islam* (Albany: State University of New York Press, 1994), p. 151.

4. Nasr, Seyyed Hossain. *Man and Nature: The Spiritual Crisis in Modern Man* (London: Unwin, 1968), p. 95.

5. Schimmel, *Deciphering,* p. 165.

6. Sells, Michael. *Approaching the Quran: The Early Revelations* (Ashland, Oreg.: White Cloud Press, 1999), pp. 11–12.

INDEX

Quest Books
are published by
The Theosophical Society in America
Wheaton, Illinois 60189-0270,
a worldwide not-for-profit, membership organization
that promotes fellowship among all peoples of the world,
encourages the study of religion, philosophy, and science,
and supports spiritual growth and healing.

Today humanity is on the verge of becoming, for the first
time in its history, a global community. The only question is
what kind of community it will be. Quest Books strives to
fulfill the purpose of the Theosophical Society to act as a
leavening; to introduce into humanity a large mindedness,
a freedom from bias, an understanding of the values of the
East and West; and to point the way to human development as a means of service, both for the individual and for
the whole of humankind.

For more information about Quest Books, visit
www.questbooks.net

For more information about the Theosophical Society, visit
www.theosophical.org, or contact Olcott@theosmail.net, or
(630) 668-1571.

The Theosophical Publishing House is aided by the generous support of the Kern Foundation, a trust dedicated to
Theosophical education.